easy
FAMILY MEALS

Cook two, eat one, freeze one – the simple
and economical way to feed your family

Linda Doeser

This edition published in 2011
LOVE FOOD is an imprint of Parragon Books Ltd

Parragon
Queen Street House
4 Queen Street
Bath BA1 1HE, UK

ISBN: 978-1-4454-3809-2

Printed in China

Cover design by Talking Design
Written by Linda Doeser
Design by Pink Creative
Photography by Clive Streeter
Food styling by Angela Drake and Teresa Goldfinch
Image on page 4 reproduced by permission of Getty Images

Notes for the Reader
This book uses both metric and imperial measurements. Follow the same units of measurement throughout; do not mix metric and imperial. All spoon measurements are level: teaspoons are assumed to be 5 ml, and tablespoons are assumed to be 15 ml. Unless otherwise stated, milk is assumed to be full fat, eggs and individual vegetables are medium, and pepper is freshly ground black pepper.

The times given are an approximate guide only. Preparation times differ according to the techniques used by different people and the cooking times may also vary from those given. Optional ingredients, variations or serving suggestions have not been included in the calculations.

Recipes using raw or very lightly cooked eggs should be avoided by infants, the elderly, pregnant women, convalescents and anyone suffering from an illness. Pregnant and breastfeeding women are advised to avoid eating peanuts and peanut products. Sufferers from nut allergies should be aware that some of the ready-made ingredients used in the recipes in this book may contain nuts. Always check the packaging before use.

Note for Parents
A few of the recipes in this book use alcoholic beverages, such as wine. Please note that some the alcohol will evaporate during the cooking process and the actual amount of alcohol remaining in a single portion of the finished dish will be low. However, if you would prefer not to serve your children dishes containing alcohol, you can replace this with the same volume of water or stock, although you will lose some depth of flavour.

Contents

Introduction

Time is tight for everyone these days, but we still want to provide tasty, nutritious, filling and healthy meals for our families. We are constantly told that the best way to do this is through home cooking using good-quality, fresh ingredients. Nevertheless, there are times when cooking from scratch just isn't an option. You might have to go out in the early evening not long after getting home from work. There might be something you feel you ought to do – whether that towering pile of ironing or a long-overdue phone call to a friend or relative – that outweighs being creative in the kitchen. Equally, there might be something that you just want to do, such as reading to young children or helping older ones with their homework. Sometimes, especially at the end of a long day, even the keenest cook simply doesn't feel like preparing the family supper.

Imagine having a freezer stocked with delicious home-cooked meals that simply need to be heated through and served, yet without spending entire weekends 'cooking for the freezer'. It may seem an impossible dream, but it can easily be turned into a reality and this book will show you how. Every recipe in the first three chapters is designed to make two meals for a family of four – one for now and one to be frozen for later. What's really good about this is that it doesn't take twice the time. Preparation will usually take a little longer – chopping two onions instead of one, for example – but this is counterbalanced by the convenience of having a frozen make-ahead meal for another day when you won't have to do any preparation at all and won't have to clear away or wash up either. Very few of the double-quantity recipes take longer to cook than a normal meal and most can be cooked in a single dish or pan.

For even greater variety, the Twice as Nice chapter suggests ways of using a basic mixture to make two different dishes. For instance, you can make two batches of meatballs and use one immediately to serve with tomato sauce and pasta, then freeze the other and use later for a scrumptious casserole. The final chapter – Love your Leftovers – provides some great ideas for making the most of leftovers. There are lots of delicious dishes than can be made with the remains of roast meats and leftover vegetables, but most of us don't want to see the same ingredients reappear later in the week. This chapter shows how easy it can be to transform these into tasty suppers that can be eaten straightaway or frozen for another day.

It is surprising how quickly make-ahead meals become a way of life. Double cooking just once or twice a week ensures an ever-changing supply of dishes for those occasions that you don't have either the time or the inclination to spend ages in the kitchen. In many families individuals frequently eat at different times, especially during the week when children are involved in a range of after-school activities. It couldn't be easier to accommodate this schedule – simply freeze dishes in individual portions so that you can thaw and reheat just what you need. Not only are these meals tastier and more nutritious than commercially available ready-meals, but also you can be certain that there is no hidden sugar, unhealthy quantities of salt or artificial colourings, preservatives and flavourings. In addition, you have all the convenience at a fraction of the cost.

There are other benefits too. You can take advantage of those supermarket promotions that make a big difference to the family budget, such as 'buy one get one free' offers. Often the extra pack is stuffed into the freezer or sits at the back of the refrigerator and stays forgotten until it is finally thrown away, but with this way of cooking family meals it is sure to be used. If you cook with seasonal produce, which is invariably cheaper than costly imported vegetables and fruit, freezing the resulting meals means that you can still enjoy it out of season.

All the recipes in this book are easy to follow and many can be prepared quickly, making them ideal for midweek meals. There are lots of suggestions for alternative ingredients so that it is easy to cook the family's favourites and to take advantage of special offers. Last, but not least, make-ahead meals make feeding your family all year round more of a pleasure and less of a chore.

Freezer Tips ❄ ❄ ❄

• If a make-ahead dish is to be frozen before cooking, never use any thawed and frozen ingredients, such as meat, fish or vegetables, in its preparation as this risks causing ill health. If the dish is to be fully cooked before it's frozen, you can safely use thawed frozen raw ingredients.

• Don't freeze warm dishes, as this will raise the temperature of the freezer.

• Cool cooked food quickly and store in the refrigerator until ready to freeze. Freeze as soon as possible.

• Pack meals into freezerproof containers with a tight-fitting lid, wrap securely in clingfilm and foil or pack into freezer bags. Always leave space for expansion when packing casseroles, stews and soups.

• Push the meat in stews and casseroles under the surface of the liquid before freezing to prevent it from drying out.

• Label the containers with the name of the dish and the date it was frozen. It is also helpful to make a list of each dish and the date as you add it to the freezer (crossing it off when you use it). Attach the list to the door or side of the freezer and check the dates regularly.

• Use the fast-freeze facility, if your freezer has one, and remember to switch it off at the appropriate time (see manufacturer's instructions).

• Some dishes can be reheated or cooked from frozen but it is usually better to thaw them first. Cover loosely and thaw at room temperature for several hours, depending on the dish, or in the refrigerator overnight.

• Thawed casseroles and stews may require a little extra liquid when reheated – about 150 ml/5 fl oz will usually be sufficient.

• Some dishes can be reheated in the microwave. Use microwaveable freezerproof containers with vented lids.

• It is better to be light-handed with spices, flavourings and seasoning as flavours intensify with freezing.

Basic Recipes

Makes 500 ml/18 fl oz

55 g/2 oz butter

55 g/2 oz plain flour

500 ml/18 fl oz warm milk

salt and pepper

White Sauce

1. Melt the butter in a saucepan. Stir in the flour and cook, stirring constantly, for 2 minutes, then gradually stir in the warm milk, a little at a time.

2. Bring to the boil, stirring constantly, then reduce the heat and simmer, stirring constantly, for 10–20 minutes, depending on how thick a consistency is required. Remove from the heat and season to taste with salt and pepper.

To freeze/reheat
When cold, transfer the sauce to a freezerproof container and freeze for up to 1 month. Thaw completely and stir well before using.

Makes 12 crêpes

115 g/4 oz plain flour

pinch of salt

1 egg, lightly beaten

300 ml/10 fl oz milk

1 tsp sunflower oil, plus extra for brushing

Crêpes

1. Sift the flour and salt into a bowl. Beat in the egg and half the milk until smooth, then stir in the remaining milk and the oil.

2. To cook, heat a 25-cm/10-inch frying pan and lightly brush with oil. Pour in a little of the batter, then tilt and rotate the pan so that it covers the base evenly. Cook for 1–1½ minutes, until the underside is golden brown. Flip over and cook the other side for 30 seconds.

3. Slide the crêpe onto a plate and repeat until all the batter has been used. Stack the cooked crêpes, interleaved with greaseproof paper, until ready to use.

To freeze/reheat

Cooked crêpes can be frozen, interleaved with greaseproof paper and sealed in a freezer bag, for up to 1 month. Thaw and reheat in a heavy-based frying pan for 1–2 minutes or simply fill while cold and bake in the oven, according to the recipe, for an extra 10 minutes.

Makes 500 g/1 lb 2 oz

500 g/1 lb 2 oz plain flour

pinch of salt

225 g/8 oz butter

iced water

Shortcrust Pastry

1. Sift the flour and salt into a bowl. Add the butter and cut it into the flour with a knife, then rub in with your fingertips until the mixture resembles fine breadcrumbs.

2. Add iced water, a little at a time, mixing with a palette knife, until the dough has a firm, rolling consistency.

3. Gather the dough into a ball, wrap in clingfilm and chill in the refrigerator for 30 minutes.

To freeze

Wrap the dough in clingfilm and foil and freeze for up to 1 month. Thaw in the refrigerator before rolling out.

To bake blind

Line the base of the uncooked pastry case with a piece of lightly greased greaseproof paper. Cover with baking beans or uncooked dried beans kept specially for the purpose and bake in a preheated oven according to the individual recipe instructions. This prevents the base of the pastry case from rising and seals it before the filling is added.

Chapter 1
Marvellous Meat & Poultry

14

18

28

Beef in Red Wine

This classic combination never fails to please and this dish would be perfect for a family celebration, yet it is surprisingly economical. Serve with mashed potatoes and a green salad for a well-balanced and tasty meal.

• •

4 tbsp plain flour

1 kg/2 lb 4 oz lean braising steak, diced

225 g/8 oz lardons or diced bacon

4 tbsp olive oil

40 g/1½ oz butter

16 baby onions or shallots

3 garlic cloves, finely chopped

225 g/8 oz mushrooms, sliced

600 ml/1 pint full-bodied red wine

175 ml/6 fl oz beef stock

1 bouquet garni

salt and pepper

mashed potatoes, to serve

fresh flat-leaf parsley sprigs, to garnish (optional)

1. Season the flour with salt and pepper to taste and toss the beef in it to coat. Shake off any excess. Heat a large flameproof casserole. Add the lardons and cook over a medium heat, stirring frequently, for 5 minutes, until golden brown. Remove with a slotted spoon.

2. Add the oil to the casserole. When it is hot, add the beef, in batches, and cook, stirring frequently, for 8–10 minutes, until browned all over. Remove with a slotted spoon. Preheat the oven to 160°C/325°F/ Gas Mark 3.

3. Melt the butter in the casserole, then add the onions and garlic and cook, stirring frequently, for 5 minutes, until light golden brown. Add the mushrooms and cook, stirring occasionally, for a further 5 minutes.

4. Return the beef and lardons to the casserole, pour in the wine and stock, add the bouquet garni and bring to the boil. Cover and transfer the casserole to the oven. Cook, stirring 2–3 times, for 1¾–2 hours, until the beef is very tender. Taste and adjust the seasoning, adding salt and pepper if needed. Remove and discard the bouquet garni. Serve half the dish immediately with mashed potatoes, garnished with parsley sprigs, if using. Leave the remainder to cool before freezing.

Variations

- If you prefer to cook without alcohol, use extra stock instead of the red wine.
- Substitute 8 chicken portions for the beef, white wine for the red wine, and chicken stock for the beef stock. Cook in a preheated oven, 180°C/350°F/Gas Mark 4, for 1 hour.
- Substitute 800 g/1 lb 12 oz pork loin steaks for the beef, dry cider for the red wine, and chicken stock for the beef stock. Cook in a preheated oven, 180°C/350°F/Gas Mark 4, for 50–60 minutes.

To freeze/reheat

When cold, transfer the reserved portion to a freezerproof container and freeze for up to 3 months. Thaw thoroughly before use, then transfer to a saucepan with a little more stock if necessary and reheat gently for 20 minutes, until piping hot.

Goulash

Most east European countries have their own recipes for this. Traditionally, it should not include flour and is not served with soured cream. However, times have changed and this modern version is just as tasty as any.

• •

4 tbsp sunflower oil

1 kg/2 lb 4 oz braising steak, trimmed and cut into cubes

1 tbsp plain flour

1 tbsp paprika, plus extra for sprinkling

600 ml/1 pint beef stock

55 g/2 oz butter

4 onions, chopped

2 carrots, diced

1½ tsp caraway seeds

1 tsp dried thyme

2 bay leaves

800 g/1 lb 12 oz canned chopped tomatoes

2 tbsp tomato purée

3 potatoes, diced

salt and pepper

soured cream, to serve (optional)

1. Preheat the oven to 160°C/325°F/Gas Mark 3. Heat the oil in a large frying pan. Add the beef, in batches, and cook over a medium heat, stirring frequently, for 8–10 minutes, until browned all over. Reduce the heat to low, sprinkle over the flour and paprika and cook, stirring constantly, for 3–4 minutes. Gradually stir in the stock and bring to the boil, stirring constantly. Remove the pan from the heat and pour the mixture into a casserole.

2. Melt the butter in the rinsed-out frying pan. Add the onions and carrots and cook over a low heat, stirring occasionally, for 5 minutes. Add the caraway seeds, thyme, bay leaves, tomatoes and tomato purée, stir well and cook for 5 minutes. Add the potatoes, season to taste with salt and pepper and bring to the boil.

3. Remove the pan from the heat and pour the mixture into the casserole. Stir, cover, transfer to the preheated oven and cook for 1¾–2 hours, until the meat is tender. Remove from the oven, taste and adjust the seasoning, adding extra salt and pepper if needed. Remove and discard the bay leaves. Serve half the goulash immediately, topped with a swirl of soured cream, if using, and a sprinkling of paprika. Leave the remainder to cool before freezing.

Variations

- You can serve this goulash with plain dumplings (see page 15) dusted with a little paprika.
- For lamb goulash, substitute trimmed and diced lamb for the braising steak and 2 red and 2 green deseeded and diced peppers for the carrots. Omit the caraway seeds and substitute 1 tbsp chopped fresh parsley for the dried thyme.

To freeze/reheat

When cold, transfer the reserved portion to a freezerproof container and freeze for up to 3 months. Thaw thoroughly before use, then transfer to a casserole, cover and reheat in a preheated oven, 180°C/350°F/Gas Mark 4, for 30 minutes, until piping hot. Alternatively, transfer to a microwave-safe dish, cover with clingfilm and pierce. Microwave according to the manufacturer's instructions, until piping hot.

Serves 4 + 4

Beef Cobbler

This tasty pie is truly a winter warmer and will satisfy even the biggest appetite. Slow cooking ensures that inexpensive braising steak is melt-in-the-mouth tender – a perfect partner for the lovely light topping.

5 tbsp sunflower oil

225 g/8 oz onions, thinly sliced

225 g/8 oz leeks, thinly sliced

4 celery sticks, sliced

1 kg/2 lb 4 oz braising steak, trimmed and cut into cubes

1 kg/2 lb 4 oz tomatoes, peeled and thickly sliced

350 ml/12 fl oz red wine, medium sherry or light beer

600 ml/1 pint beef stock

3 tbsp chopped fresh parsley

salt and pepper

Cobbler Topping

350 g/12 oz self-raising flour, plus extra for dusting

pinch of salt

55 g/2 oz butter, diced

200–350 ml/7–12 fl oz milk

1. Preheat the oven to 160°C/325°F/Gas Mark 3. Heat the oil in a flameproof casserole. Add the onions, leeks and celery and cook over a low heat, stirring occasionally, for 5 minutes, until softened. Add the beef, in batches, increase the heat to medium and cook, stirring frequently, for 8–10 minutes, until lightly browned all over.

2. Add the tomatoes and cook, stirring occasionally, for 2–3 minutes, then pour in the wine and cook for a few minutes until the alcohol has evaporated. Pour in the stock and stir well. Season to taste with salt and pepper and stir in the parsley. Bring to the boil, then cover and transfer to the preheated oven. Cook for 1¾–2 hours, until the meat is tender.

3. Meanwhile, make the topping. Sift together the flour and salt into a bowl, then add the butter and rub in with your fingertips. Gradually stir in enough milk to make a soft dough.

4. Roll out the dough on a lightly floured surface to about 15 mm/⅝ inch thick and stamp out 16 rounds with a plain biscuit cutter. Put half the rounds in a freezerproof container, interleaving the layers with greaseproof paper, and chill in the refrigerator until ready to freeze.

5. Remove the casserole from the oven and increase the oven temperature to 200°C/400°F/Gas Mark 6. Transfer half the beef mixture to a bowl and leave to cool before freezing. Put the remaining dough rounds on top of the remaining beef mixture, return the casserole, without the lid, to the oven and cook for a further 15–20 minutes, until the topping is golden brown. Serve immediately.

Variations

- If you prefer to cook without alcohol, use extra stock instead of the red wine, sherry or beer.
- Substitute dumplings (cannot be frozen) for the cobbler topping. Sift together 115 g/4 oz self-raising flour and a pinch of salt and stir in 55 g/2 oz shredded suet and 2 tbsp chopped fresh parsley. Stir in just enough water to make a soft dough. Shape into small balls and add to the casserole at the start of step 5, but do not increase the oven temperature. Cook for a further 25–30 minutes.

To freeze/reheat

When cold, transfer the reserved beef mixture to a freezerproof container. Freeze the beef mixture and dough rounds for up to 3 months. Thaw thoroughly before use, then heat the beef mixture in a casserole in a preheated oven, 180°C/350°F/Gas Mark 4, for 20 minutes. Increase the temperature to 200°C/400°F/Gas Mark 6, top with the dough rounds and bake for a further 15–20 minutes, until piping hot.

Beef Burgers

1 kg/2 lb 4 oz fresh steak mince

1 small onion, grated

40 g/1½ oz fresh breadcrumbs

½ tsp dried thyme

1 large egg

Lamb Burgers

1 kg/2 lb 4 oz fresh lamb mince

1 small onion, grated

40 g/1½ oz fresh breadcrumbs

1 large egg

2 tbsp chopped fresh mint

Chicken or Turkey Burgers

1 kg/2 lb 4 oz fresh chicken or turkey mince

1 small onion, grated

40 g/1½ oz fresh breadcrumbs

3–4 tbsp soured cream

2 tbsp chopped fresh basil

salt and pepper

sunflower oil, for brushing

To Serve

4 burger buns, split and toasted

lettuce leaves

tomato slices

sauces or relishes of your choice

The Best Burgers

Everyone loves burgers, but once you have tried any of these home-made versions you'll never buy ready-made ones again. Choose from beef, lamb, chicken or turkey burgers – each recipe makes enough for 8 burgers.

1. Mix together your chosen burger ingredients in a bowl until thoroughly combined. Season to taste with salt and pepper. Divide into 8 equal-sized pieces and shape each into a patty.

2. Transfer the patties to a plate and chill in the refrigerator for 30 minutes to firm them up before cooking, if you have time.

3. Brush 4 of the patties with oil and cook under a preheated grill or on the barbecue for about 5 minutes on each side, turning them carefully (home-made burgers are more fragile than ready-made ones), or until cooked through. Place them in the toasted buns and serve with lettuce, tomatoes and your chosen sauces or relishes.

Variation

- For special cheese burgers, divide the burger mixture into 16. Shape half into patties and divide 115 g/4 oz crumbled Stilton, feta, Lancashire or Caerphilly cheese among them. Shape the remaining pieces into patties, put them on top of the cheese and gently mould with your hands until the cheese is completely enclosed.

To freeze/reheat

Wrap the remaining burgers individually and freeze for up to 3 months. Thaw thoroughly, then cook and serve as described in step 3.

Serves 4 + 4

40 g/1½ oz butter

1 onion, finely chopped

2 celery sticks, finely chopped

1 carrot, finely chopped

500 g/1 lb 2 oz fresh steak mince

500 g/1 lb 2 oz fresh pork mince

70 g/2½ oz fresh breadcrumbs

2 large eggs, lightly beaten

3 tbsp chopped mixed fresh herbs

4 tbsp tomato ketchup

3 tbsp Worcestershire sauce

12 bacon slices

salt and pepper

fresh flat-leaf parsley sprigs,
to garnish

Meat Loaf

Easy to slice and less expensive than a roast, meat loaf is delicious served hot and, should there be any leftovers, it is great for a packed lunch the following day. This is a wonderfully flexible recipe with many variations.

1. Preheat the oven to 180°C/350°F/Gas Mark 4. Melt the butter in a frying pan. Add the onion, celery and carrot and cook over a low heat, stirring occasionally, for 5 minutes, until softened. Remove from the heat and leave to cool.

2. Transfer the vegetables to a large bowl and add the meat, breadcrumbs, eggs, herbs, tomato ketchup and Worcestershire sauce. Season well with salt and pepper and mix together gently until thoroughly combined.

3. Divide the mixture in half and shape each piece into a loaf shape with dampened hands. Line the bases and sides of 2 x 900-g/2-lb loaf tins with the bacon, then press the meat loaf filling into the prepared tins.

4. Put 1 loaf into the preheated oven and cook for 1¼–1½ hours, until cooked through. Cover the other loaf with clingfilm and store in the refrigerator until ready to freeze.

5. Remove the tin from the oven and drain off the fat. Cover the loaf with foil and leave to rest for 10 minutes, then carefully transfer to a warmed serving dish. Cut into slices, garnish with parsley sprigs and serve immediately.

Variations

- Substitute 200 g/7 oz finely chopped mushrooms for the celery or 6 peeled and diced tomatoes for the celery and carrots.
- Replace 225 g/8 oz of the pork mince with the same quantity of grated Cheddar cheese or finely chopped ham.
- Substitute chilli sauce for the tomato ketchup.

To freeze/reheat

Wrap the chilled loaf in clingfilm and foil or a freezer bag and freeze for up to 3 months. Thaw thoroughly, then cook in a preheated oven, 180°C/350°F/Gas Mark 4, for 1¼–1½ hours, until piping hot.

French Bacon Soup

This meal-in-a-bowl soup is warming and very satisfying when served with crusty bread. You can vary the vegetables, depending on what is in season, but make sure that you cut them all to the same size so that they cook evenly.

1 kg/2 lb 4 oz boneless boiling bacon, trimmed of fat

4 onions, chopped

8 carrots, diced

4–6 turnips, diced

10 potatoes, diced

500 g/1 lb 2 oz shelled peas

500 g/1 lb 2 oz shelled broad beans

1 green cabbage, coarse leaves removed, shredded

salt and pepper

1. If you're not sure how salty the bacon is, soak it in water to cover overnight, then drain. Put the bacon into a large saucepan, pour in water to cover and bring to the boil over a medium heat. Skim off the foam that rises to the surface, then reduce the heat, partially cover the pan and simmer for 1 hour.

2. Add the onions, carrots, turnips and potatoes, then cover and simmer for 30 minutes. Add the peas and beans, cover and simmer for a further 20 minutes. Season to taste with salt and pepper, bearing in mind that the bacon is still likely to be quite salty. Add the cabbage and simmer for 5 minutes.

3. Remove the piece of bacon and dice the meat. Return it to the pan and cook for 2 minutes. Ladle half the soup into bowls and serve. Leave the remainder to cool before freezing.

Variations

- For an even more substantial soup, add 500 g/1 lb 2 oz rustic French sausages (saucisses de campagne) with the root vegetables in step 2. (You could then reduce the amount of bacon if you like.)
- For a winter soup, substitute cooked or canned lentils for the peas, and haricot or butter beans for the broad beans.
- If using bacon on the bone, which is more of a nuisance to cut up but just as tasty, double the weight.

To freeze/reheat

When cold, chill the reserved soup in the refrigerator, then lift off and discard any fat that has set on the surface. Transfer to a freezerproof container and freeze for up to 3 months. Thaw thoroughly, then transfer to a saucepan and reheat until piping hot. You can also reheat it in the microwave.

Serves 4 + 4

Pork & Peppers

This easy one-pot dish can be cooked on the hob or in the oven. It's delicious served with rice or noodles or, if you cook it in the oven, with baked potatoes for a filling and economical supper.

- -

4 tbsp olive or sunflower oil

8 pork chops or 24 slices of pork fillet

2 large onions, sliced

3 garlic cloves, finely chopped

2 red peppers, deseeded and sliced

425 g/15 oz canned sweetcorn

2 tsp chopped fresh sage, plus extra leaves to garnish

150 ml/5 fl oz chicken or vegetable stock or white wine, if needed

salt and pepper

freshly cooked egg noodles or rice, to serve

1. If you are going to cook this dish in the oven, preheat it to 200°C/400°F/Gas Mark 6. Heat the oil in a flameproof casserole. Add the pork, in batches if necessary, and cook over a medium heat, turning occasionally, for 8–10 minutes, until lightly browned on both sides. Remove with tongs and set aside.

2. Add the onions and garlic to the casserole, reduce the heat to low and cook, stirring occasionally, for 5 minutes, until softened. Add the peppers and cook, stirring occasionally, for a further 5 minutes, then stir in the sweetcorn with its can juices and the sage. Season to taste with salt and pepper, then return the meat to the casserole.

3. Stir well, cover and simmer for 30 minutes, until the pork is tender. If it seems to be drying out, add some or all of the stock. Alternatively, transfer the covered casserole to the preheated oven and bake for 45 minutes, adding a little stock if necessary. Transfer half the meat and vegetables to warmed plates, garnish with sage leaves and serve immediately with cooked noodles or rice. Leave the remainder to cool before freezing.

Variation

- For a spicy version, marinate the pork in a mixture of 4 tbsp olive oil, 1 tbsp paprika, ½ tsp ground cinnamon and 1½ tsp ground ginger for 45–60 minutes before cooking. Substitute drained canned chickpeas for the sweetcorn, 2 tbsp chopped fresh parsley for the sage, increase the quantity of stock to 225–300 ml/8–10 fl oz and add 175 g/ 6 oz chopped ready-to-eat dried apricots.

To freeze/reheat

When cold, transfer the reserved meat and vegetables to a freezerproof container and freeze for up to 3 months. Thaw thoroughly, then transfer to a saucepan, cover and reheat gently over a low heat, stirring occasionally, for about 20 minutes, until piping hot.

Serves 4 + 4

Lamb Tagine

This luscious North African stew features the complementary flavours of lamb and dried fruit combined with a subtle mix of warming spices. Serve with couscous or rice for a filling meal.

4 tbsp olive oil

1.3 kg/3 lb diced lamb

1 tsp ground cinnamon

1 tsp ground ginger

1 tsp ground turmeric

2 tsp ground cumin

2 Spanish onions, finely chopped

2 garlic cloves, finely chopped

finely grated rind of ½ lemon

1.3 litres/2¼ pints water

500 g/1 lb 2 oz okra, trimmed

280 g/10 oz ready-to-eat dried apricots or prunes, quartered

150 g/5½ oz blanched almonds, toasted

2 tbsp clear honey

3 tbsp chopped fresh coriander

1. Heat the oil in a large saucepan. Add the lamb, cinnamon, ginger, turmeric and cumin and cook over a medium heat, stirring frequently, for 8–10 minutes, until the lamb is lightly browned all over. Remove with a slotted spoon.

2. Add the onions and garlic, reduce the heat to low and cook, stirring occasionally, for 5 minutes, until softened. Add the lemon rind, return the lamb to the pan and pour in the water. Stir well, increase the heat and bring to the boil, then reduce the heat, cover and simmer for 1 hour.

3. Add the okra, apricots, almonds, honey and coriander. Simmer, uncovered, for a further 30–40 minutes, until everything is tender. Transfer half the tagine to a warmed serving dish. Leave the remainder to cool before freezing.

Variations

- For a hotter flavour, add a large pinch of chilli flakes with the other spices.
- For an even fruitier flavour, stir in the finely chopped rind of 1 preserved lemon in step 3 and omit the grated lemon rind. (Lemons preserved in salt are available from supermarkets; rinse well and discard the flesh.)
- Substitute 1 tsp ground coriander for 1 tsp of the cumin and 3 diced aubergines for the okra.

To freeze/reheat

When cold, transfer the reserved tagine to a freezerproof container and freeze for up to 3 months. Thaw thoroughly, then transfer to a saucepan and reheat gently, stirring occasionally, until piping hot.

Mediterranean Chicken

A colourful medley of sun-ripened vegetables guarantees that the chicken will be succulent and full of flavour. Not only is this a really delicious dish, but it is also healthy and packed with nutrients.

4 tbsp olive oil

8 skinless, boneless chicken breasts or 16 skinless chicken thighs, diced

2 onions, chopped

3 garlic cloves, finely chopped

4 courgettes, halved lengthways and sliced

2 aubergines, diced

2 red peppers, deseeded and diced

2 green peppers, deseeded and diced

800 g/1 lb 12 oz canned chopped tomatoes

pinch of saffron threads, crushed (optional)

4 tbsp chopped fresh flat-leaf parsley, plus extra sprigs to garnish

salt and pepper

freshly cooked rice, to serve

1. Heat the oil in a large saucepan. Add the chicken and cook over a medium heat, turning once or twice, for 8–10 minutes, until lightly browned all over. Remove from the pan and set aside.

2. Add the onions and garlic, reduce the heat and cook, stirring occasionally, for 5 minutes, until softened. Stir in the courgettes, aubergines and red and green peppers and cook over a medium heat, stirring occasionally, for a further 5 minutes. Add the tomatoes, saffron, if using, and parsley. Season to taste with salt and pepper, then bring to the boil.

3. Return the chicken to the pan, reduce the heat to low, cover and simmer for 45–50 minutes, or until the chicken is cooked through and tender. Transfer half the chicken and vegetables to warmed plates, garnish with parsley sprigs and serve immediately with rice. Leave the remainder to cool before freezing.

Variations

- For a spicier version, cook 800 g/1 lb 12 oz diced chicken as in step 1 and add 115 g/4 oz diced chorizo to the pan with the courgettes, aubergines and peppers in step 2. Substitute 1 tsp smoked paprika for the saffron. Simmer for 30–40 minutes, until tender.
- Substitute 900 g/2 lb diced pork for the chicken in the main recipe or 800 g/1 lb 12 oz diced pork in the spicy version.

To freeze/reheat

When cold, transfer the reserved chicken and vegetables to a freezerproof container and freeze for up to 3 months. Thaw thoroughly, then transfer to a saucepan and reheat gently for 20–30 minutes, until piping hot.

Thai Green Curry

This creamy curry is very quick and easy to make and is delicious served with rice or noodles. Jars of green curry paste are available from most supermarkets and are generally of very good quality.

• •

1 lemon grass stalk

3 tbsp groundnut oil

3 tbsp Thai green curry paste

900 g/2 lb skinless, boneless chicken breasts, cut into thin strips

grated rind of 1 lime or 6 kaffir lime leaves

425 ml/15 fl oz canned coconut milk

3 tbsp Thai fish sauce

300 g/10½ oz canned bamboo shoots, drained and rinsed

fresh basil leaves and sliced green chillies, to garnish

freshly cooked egg noodles or rice, to serve

1. Bruise the bulb of the lemon grass with the back of a kitchen knife, then finely chop it and the first 10 cm/4 inches of the stalk. Discard the remainder.

2. Heat the oil in a large frying pan. Add the curry paste and cook over a low heat, stirring constantly, until it gives off its aroma and is bubbling. Add the chicken, chopped lemon grass and the lime rind, increase the heat to medium and cook, stirring frequently, for 4–5 minutes, until the chicken is lightly browned.

3. Stir in the coconut milk and bring to the boil, then reduce the heat and simmer for 10 minutes, until the chicken is tender. Stir in the fish sauce and bamboo shoots and cook for a further 2–3 minutes.

4. Transfer half the curry to warmed plates, garnish with basil leaves and chillies and serve immediately with noodles or rice. Leave the remainder to cool before freezing.

Variations

- Peel and devein 900 g/2 lb raw tiger prawns and substitute them for the chicken. Cook for 2–3 minutes in step 2, until they turn pink, and simmer for 5 minutes in step 3. Freeze for up to 1 month.
- Substitute the same quantity of rump steak strips for the chicken and canned straw mushrooms for the bamboo shoots.

To freeze/reheat

When cold, transfer the reserved curry to a freezerproof container and freeze for up to 3 months. Thaw thoroughly, then transfer to a saucepan and reheat gently for 15 minutes, until piping hot.

Chapter 2
Fabulous Fish & Seafood

34

36

46

Fish Cakes

Easy to make and even easier to eat, fish cakes are popular with all the family. Even children who may refuse other fish dishes usually like them. You can use almost any white fish you like.

Serves 4 + 4

1.8 kg/4 lb floury potatoes, cut into pieces

2 kg/4 lb 8 oz white fish fillets, skinned

55 g/2 oz butter

5 tbsp chopped fresh parsley

115 g/4 oz plain flour

3 large eggs

280 g/10 oz fresh breadcrumbs

vegetable oil, for deep-frying

salt and pepper

potato wedges and salad, to serve

1. Put the potatoes into a saucepan, pour in water to cover, add a pinch of salt and bring to the boil. Reduce the heat, cover and simmer for 20–25 minutes, until tender. Drain, return to the pan and mash until smooth. Leave to cool.

2. Meanwhile, put the fish into a wide pan, pour in water to cover and bring to the boil. Reduce the heat, cover and poach for 10 minutes, until the flesh flakes easily. Lift out with a fish slice, transfer to a chopping board and leave until cool enough to handle. Flake the flesh, removing any pin bones.

3. Melt the butter in a saucepan over a low heat. Mix together the mashed potatoes, flaked fish, melted butter and parsley in a bowl and season to taste with salt and pepper. Using your hands, shape the mixture into 16 rounds, then flatten into patties. Put them onto a plate, cover with clingfilm and chill in the refrigerator for 30 minutes.

4. Put the flour into a shallow dish, season to taste with salt and pepper and mix well. Beat the eggs in another shallow dish and spread out the breadcrumbs in a third. Preheat the oil in a deep-fat fryer to 180–190°C/350–375°F, or until a cube of bread browns in 30 seconds. Meanwhile, remove the fish cakes from the refrigerator and uncover.

5. Dip the fish cakes in the flour, then in the eggs and, finally, in the breadcrumbs, pressing them on with your fingers. Return half the fish cakes to the refrigerator until ready to freeze. Add the remaining fish cakes to the hot oil, in batches, and deep-fry for 4–5 minutes, until golden brown. Lift out with a fish slice, drain on kitchen paper and serve immediately with potato wedges and salad.

Variations

- Substitute salmon fillets for the white fish, halve the quantity of parsley and add 1 tbsp chopped fresh dill.
- Reduce the quantity of white fish fillets to 1.3 kg/3 lb and add 280 g/10 oz chopped smoked salmon in step 3.
- For a Thai flavour, add 2½ tbsp Thai red curry paste and 2 tbsp Thai fish sauce to the mixture in step 3 and replace the parsley with fresh coriander.

To freeze/reheat

Wrap the reserved fish cakes individually in clingfilm and foil and freeze for up to 1 month. Thaw thoroughly, then cook as described in step 5.

Serves 4 + 4

Fish Pie

Fish pie is a hearty and tasty way of serving fish but it's one of those dishes that seems to require just about every utensil in the kitchen. This way you have two meals but only one session of clearing up.

1.3 kg/3 lb white fish fillets

1.3 kg/3 lb potatoes, cut into chunks

175 g/6 oz butter

1 Spanish onion or 2 onions, chopped

55 g/2 oz plain flour

300 ml/10 fl oz warm milk, plus extra for mashing

4 hard-boiled eggs, chopped

3 tbsp chopped fresh parsley

1 tbsp lemon juice

dash of Tabasco sauce or pinch of cayenne pepper

115 g/4 oz Cheddar or other semi-hard cheese, grated

salt and pepper

1. Put the fish into a large pan, pour in water to cover. Season to taste with salt and pepper, cover and bring to the boil. Reduce the heat and poach for 12–15 minutes, until the flesh flakes easily. Remove from the heat and transfer the fish to a chopping board. Reserve 300 ml/ 10 fl oz of the cooking liquid.

2. Put the potatoes into a saucepan, pour in cold water to cover and add a pinch of salt. Cover and bring to the boil, then reduce the heat and simmer for 20–25 minutes, until tender.

3. Meanwhile, melt 55 g/2 oz of the butter in a frying pan. Add the onion and cook over a low heat, stirring occasionally, for 5 minutes, until softened. Remove the pan from the heat.

4. Drain the potatoes and return to the pan. Add 55 g/2 oz of the remaining butter and mash well, adding as much milk as necessary for a creamy consistency. Leave to cool.

5. Meanwhile, remove the skin and any remaining bones from the fish and flake the flesh. Preheat the oven to 200°C/400°F/Gas Mark 6.

6. Melt the remaining butter in a saucepan. Stir in the flour and cook, stirring constantly, for 2 minutes, then gradually stir in the milk and the reserved cooking liquid, a little at a time. Bring to the boil, stirring constantly, then reduce the heat and simmer, stirring constantly, for 10–20 minutes, until thickened. Stir in the fish, onion, eggs, parsley, lemon juice and Tabasco and season to taste with salt and pepper.

7. Spoon the mixture into 2 ovenproof dishes, dividing it equally between them, and smooth the surface. Spoon the potato on top and smooth with a palette knife. Sprinkle half the cheese evenly over the surface of each.

8. Set 1 dish aside to cool before freezing. Put the other dish on a baking sheet and bake in the preheated oven for 30 minutes, until lightly browned. Serve immediately.

Variations

- Substitute 450 g/1 lb cooked peeled prawns for the same quantity of fish fillets. Stir them into the sauce in step 6 with the cooked fish and flavourings.
- Drain 400 g/14 oz canned sweetcorn and add to the sauce in step 6 instead of the hard-boiled eggs.
- Replace half the quantity of potatoes with celeriac or parsnips.

To freeze/reheat

When cold, wrap the reserved pie in clingfilm and foil and freeze for up to 1 month. Thaw thoroughly, then cook in a preheated oven, 200°C/400°F/Gas Mark 6, for 30 minutes, until piping hot.

Serves 4 + 4

Fish in Tomato Sauce

Fish fillets with a breadcrumb coating are widely available and often feature as supermarket 'specials', making them a very economical purchase. Make them a bit more exciting by baking them in a tasty but simple sauce.

3 tbsp olive oil

8 fish fillets in breadcrumbs, thawed if frozen

1 large onion, finely chopped

4–5 garlic cloves, finely chopped

2 tbsp tomato purée

1 tbsp water

800 g/1 lb 12 oz canned chopped tomatoes

1 tsp sugar

3 tbsp chopped fresh parsley or 1 tsp dried thyme

salt and pepper

freshly cooked green vegetables, to serve

1. Preheat the oven to 180°C/350°F/Gas Mark 4. Heat the oil in a large frying pan. Add the fish fillets, in batches if necessary, and cook over a low–medium heat for 2 minutes on each side, until lightly browned. Remove from the pan with a fish slice and put into a large ovenproof dish in a single layer.

2. Add the onion and garlic to the pan and cook, stirring occasionally, for 5 minutes, until softened. Mix the tomato purée with the water and add to the pan with the tomatoes and sugar. Season to taste with salt and pepper and bring to the boil, then reduce the heat and simmer for 10 minutes, until thickened. Stir in the parsley.

3. Pour the sauce over the fish to cover it completely. Cover the dish with foil and bake in the preheated oven for 25–30 minutes, until the fish flakes easily.

4. Transfer half the sauce-coated fish to serving plates and serve immediately with green vegetables. Leave the remainder to cool before freezing.

Variations

- You could also use 16–24 breaded fish fingers instead of fillets. This is especially popular with children.
- Substitute breaded turkey steaks for the fish.
- If you're not a garlic enthusiast, reduce the number of cloves, or omit them completely, and add 200 g/7 oz finely chopped mushrooms after softening the onion in step 2. Cook, stirring frequently, for 5 minutes before adding the tomato purée.

To freeze/reheat

When cold, transfer the reserved fish and sauce to a freezerproof container and freeze for up to 1 month. Thaw thoroughly, then transfer to an ovenproof dish and reheat in a preheated oven, 180°C/350°F/Gas Mark 4, for 15–20 minutes, until piping hot. You can also reheat it in the microwave.

Salmon & Broccoli Pies

These charming little pies with a crisp golden pastry crust will appeal to all members of the family. Children's smaller appetites may be satisfied with a single pie, while adults will probably enjoy a serving of two.

250 g/9 oz broccoli, cut into florets

250 g/9 oz salmon fillets

1 quantity White Sauce
(see page 6)

1 quantity Shortcrust Pastry
(see page 7) or 725 g/1 lb 9½ oz
shop-bought shortcrust pastry

plain flour, for dusting

1 egg yolk

1 tbsp water

salt and pepper

salad, to serve

1. Cook the broccoli in a pan of lightly salted boiling water or steam for 10–15 minutes, until tender. Remove from the heat, drain and leave to cool.

2. Bring a wide pan of lightly salted water to the boil, then reduce the heat so that the surface barely shivers. Add the fish and poach, turning halfway through cooking, for 5 minutes, until the flesh flakes easily. Remove with a fish slice and leave to cool.

3. Remove and discard the skin and flake the flesh, removing any bones. Place in a bowl. Break the broccoli florets into small pieces over the bowl, using your fingers. Finely chop the stems, discarding any thick ones, and add to the bowl. Add the white sauce, season to taste with salt and pepper and mix well. Cover and place in the refrigerator until required.

4. Roll out the pastry on a lightly floured surface to a thin sheet. Stamp out 32 rounds with a 10-cm/4-inch biscuit cutter. Put rounds, in batches, into a Yorkshire pudding tin or deep tartlet tin. Add spoonfuls of the salmon mixture to the holes without filling them completely. Brush the edges of the same number of rounds with water and put them on top. Press together with the tines of a fork to seal and remove from the tin. Repeat with the remaining rounds to make 16 pies. Chill in the refrigerator for 30 minutes.

5. Preheat the oven to 200°C/400°F/Gas Mark 6. Beat the egg yolk with the water in a cup. Transfer the required number of pies for a single meal to a baking sheet, brush with the egg yolk to glaze and bake in the preheated oven for 20–25 minutes, until golden brown. Serve immediately with salad.

Variations

- Substitute fresh or smoked white fish fillets for the salmon and drained canned sweetcorn for the broccoli.
- Substitute diced cooked chicken for the salmon and drained and chopped red peppers preserved in oil for the broccoli.
- Stir 2 tsp sun-dried tomato paste into the white sauce before adding it to the fish.

To freeze/reheat

Wrap the reserved uncooked pies individually in clingfilm and foil and freeze for up to 1 month. Thaw thoroughly, then glaze with diluted egg yolk and cook in a preheated oven, 200°C/400°F/ Gas Mark 6, for 20–25 minutes, until piping hot.

Fish Gratin

This creamy dish is quick and easy to prepare and tastes fabulous. You can make the gratins in large dishes or individual ones. Freezing individual servings is ideal for families who don't always eat together or where one family member dislikes fish.

butter, for greasing

8 tomatoes, skinned and diced

900 g/2 lb firm white fish fillets, skinned and cut into chunks

450 g/1 lb cooked peeled prawns

200 g/7 oz Cheddar or Gruyère cheese, grated

6 spring onions, finely chopped

400 ml/14 fl oz double cream

salt and pepper

1. Preheat the oven to 220°C/425°F/Gas Mark 7. Grease 2 large ovenproof dishes or 8 individual gratin dishes with butter.

2. Divide the tomatoes equally among the dishes, sprinkling them over the bases. Cover with the fish and prawns, then sprinkle with the cheese and spring onions. Pour the cream over the top.

3. Put the dishes onto baking sheets and bake in the preheated oven for 20–30 minutes (depending on the size of the dishes), until the topping is golden brown and bubbling. Remove from the oven and serve 1 large gratin or 4 individual ones immediately. Leave the remainder to cool before freezing.

Variations

- Substitute cooked shelled mussels (available in vacuum packs from supermarkets) for the prawns, and 2 tbsp snipped chives and 1 tbsp chopped fresh dill for the spring onions.
- Substitute a freshwater fish, such as trout or tilapia, for the white fish fillets.

To freeze/reheat

When cold, wrap the reserved gratins in clingfilm and foil and freeze for up to 1 month. Thaw thoroughly, then cook in a preheated oven, 180°C/350°F/Gas Mark 4, for 10–15 minutes, until piping hot.

Clam Chowder

This famous American soup is really more of a stew, deriving its name from the French word for a stew pot. It's traditionally made with large clams called quahogs, but you can use whatever type is easily available.

• •

1 tbsp corn oil

115 g/4 oz bacon, diced

40 g/1½ oz butter

2 onions, chopped

3 potatoes, diced

3 celery sticks, chopped

3 leeks, sliced

600 g/1 lb 5 oz canned chopped tomatoes

4 tbsp chopped fresh parsley

1.7 litres/3 pints fish stock

1.2 kg/2 lb 12 oz carpet shell or Venus clams

300 ml/10 fl oz water

salt and pepper

crusty bread, to serve

1. Heat the oil in a large saucepan. Add the bacon and cook over a low–medium heat, stirring frequently, for 6–8 minutes, until crisp. Remove with a slotted spoon.

2. Melt the butter in a pan. Add the onions, potatoes and celery, then season to taste with salt. Reduce the heat to low, cover and cook, stirring occasionally, for 10 minutes, until thoroughly softened but not coloured. Add the leeks, tomatoes and 3 tablespoons of the parsley. Pour in the stock, stir well and bring to the boil over a medium heat. Reduce the heat, cover and simmer gently for 10 minutes, until the vegetables are tender.

3. Meanwhile, scrub the clams under cold running water and discard any with broken shells and any that refuse to close when tapped. Put them into a separate saucepan and pour in the water. Cover and cook over a high heat, shaking the pan occasionally, for 4–5 minutes, until the shells open.

4. Remove the clams with a slotted spoon and discard any that remain closed. Strain the cooking liquid through a muslin-lined strainer into the chowder. Remove the clams from their shells.

5. Season the chowder to taste with salt and pepper and stir in the clams. Ladle half the chowder into warmed soup plates, then sprinkle with the bacon and the remaining parsley and serve with crusty bread. Leave the remaining soup to cool before freezing.

Variations

- For New England clam chowder, omit the tomatoes and substitute milk or a mixture of milk and double cream for the fish stock.
- You can replace some or all of the clams with other shellfish or a mixture of shellfish and chunks of white fish fillet.

To freeze/reheat

When cold, ladle the reserved soup into a freezerproof container and freeze for up to 1 month. Thaw thoroughly, then transfer to a saucepan and reheat gently, stirring occasionally, until piping hot. Meanwhile, cook 115 g/4 oz diced bacon as described in step 1. Serve the soup, garnished with the bacon and 1 tbsp chopped fresh parsley.

Serves 4 + 4

Baked Salmon Parcels

There are lots of advantages to cooking fish in parcels – less clearing up afterwards, a reduction in lingering odours and everybody enjoys unwrapping them at the table. Do not use fish that has previously been frozen for this dish.

olive oil, for brushing and drizzling

1 large onion, thinly sliced

2 garlic cloves, finely chopped

4 tomatoes, sliced

8 salmon fillets, about 140 g/
5 oz each

4 red peppers, deseeded and
sliced

salt and pepper

freshly cooked green beans,
to serve

Creamy Pesto Sauce

4 tbsp red pepper pesto

150 ml/5 fl oz crème fraîche

1. Preheat the oven to 200°C/400°F/Gas Mark 6. Cut out 8 foil and 8 greaseproof paper squares measuring 38 cm/15 inches. Put the paper squares on top of the foil ones and brush with oil.

2. Divide the onion, garlic and tomatoes among the squares, placing them almost in the middle. Season the fish to taste with salt and pepper and put a fish fillet on top of each pile of vegetables. Divide the red pepper among the parcels and drizzle with a little oil.

3. Fold the squares of foil and paper over the fish, then fold over 1 cm/½ inch of the open edge, working your way all around to make a half moon shape. Repeat the process to seal the edge securely.

4. Put 4 parcels in the refrigerator until ready to freeze. Put the remaining parcels on a baking sheet and bake in the preheated oven for 20 minutes. Meanwhile, stir the pesto into the crème fraîche in a small bowl.

5. When the parcels have puffed up, remove them from the oven. Transfer to a warmed serving dish, slit the top with a sharp knife and pull back the paper and foil. Serve immediately with green beans and the creamy pesto sauce.

Variations

- For salmon with artichokes, replace the peppers with 8 drained and sliced chargrilled artichokes in oil. Drizzle the fish with a little oil from the jar. Substitute white artichoke pesto for the red pepper pesto to serve.
- Substitute fresh white fish fillets for the salmon, 3–4 sliced courgettes for the tomatoes and 8 stoned olives and 8 drained capers for the peppers. Serve with ready-made tapenade.

To freeze/reheat

Carefully pack the reserved uncooked parcels into a freezer bag, seal and freeze for up to 1 month. Thaw thoroughly, then cook in a preheated oven, 200°C/400°F/Gas Mark 6, for 20 minutes, until piping hot. Serve with freshly made creamy pesto sauce.

Smoked Salmon Quiche

This luxurious treat need not be expensive if you buy smoked salmon trimmings. These misshapen pieces still taste wonderful and they're going to be cut up anyway so their irregularity really doesn't matter.

● ●

¾ quantity Shortcrust Pastry (see page 7) or 550 g/1 lb 4 oz shop-bought shortcrust pastry

plain flour, for dusting

8 eggs

600 ml/1 pint double cream

2 tbsp finely chopped fresh dill

200 g/7 oz Cheddar cheese, grated

350 g/12 oz smoked salmon, cut into small pieces

pepper

1. Preheat the oven to 190°C/375°F/Gas Mark 5. Divide the pastry in half, then roll out each piece on a lightly floured surface and use it to line a 23-cm/9-inch quiche tin or dish. Bake blind (see page 7) in the preheated oven for 15 minutes, until the dough is just set and light golden.

2. Meanwhile, beat the eggs with the cream and dill in a bowl. Season to taste with pepper.

3. Remove the pastry cases from the oven and remove the foil and beans. Divide the cheese between them, sprinkling it evenly over the bases. Divide the smoked salmon evenly between them, then ladle the egg and cream mixture into the pastry cases, but do not overfill. Reserve any leftover mixture.

4. Bake for 25–30 minutes, checking the depth of filling halfway through the cooking time. If the filling has sunk as it sets, add any remaining egg and cream mixture and return the quiches to the oven.

5. When the filling, including the centre, is set and golden and the pastry cases are lightly browned, remove the quiches from the oven. If you like, you can serve 1 hot or leave both to cool for serving cold or for freezing.

Variations

- For Quiche Lorraine, substitute 200 g/7 oz cooked diced bacon for the smoked salmon.
- For a vegetarian filling, substitute 8 sliced courgettes and 10 small peeled and sliced tomatoes for the salmon. Use a pinch of dried oregano instead of the dill.
- For a mushroom quiche, cook 4 finely chopped shallots in a little butter for 5 minutes, then add 900 g/2 lb thinly sliced mushrooms and cook for a further 5 minutes. Use in place of the smoked salmon.

To freeze/reheat

When cold, remove the quiche from the tin, if you like. Put it into a freezer bag and freeze for up to 3 months. Thaw thoroughly and serve cold.

Chapter 3
Vibrant Veggies

Aubergine Crêpes

Filled crêpes coated with a tasty cheese sauce are – well, very filling – and a sure-fire hit with all the family. Not only delicious and nutritious, this is a very economical dish that's a bit messy and time-consuming, but incredibly easy.

900 g/2 lb aubergines, diced

2 quantities Crêpe Batter (see page 7)

5 tbsp sunflower oil, plus extra for brushing

2 onions, sliced

900 g/2 lb tomatoes, peeled and diced

280 g/10 oz Gruyère cheese, grated

1 tsp dried mixed herbs

butter, for greasing

1 tbsp Dijon mustard

1 quantity hot White Sauce (see page 6)

25 g/1 oz Parmesan cheese, grated

salt and pepper

salad leaves, to serve

1. Put the aubergines into a colander, sprinkling each layer with salt, and leave to drain for 30 minutes. Rinse under cold running water and pat dry with kitchen paper.

2. Meanwhile, heat a 25-cm/10-inch frying pan and lightly brush with oil. Pour in a little of the crêpe batter, then tilt and rotate the pan so that it covers the base evenly. Cook for 1–1½ minutes, until the underside is golden brown. Flip over and cook the second side for 30 seconds. Slide the crêpe onto a plate and repeat until all the batter has been used. Stack the cooked crêpes, interleaved with greaseproof paper, and keep warm.

3. Heat half the oil in a large frying pan. Add the aubergines and cook over a low–medium heat, stirring frequently, for 10 minutes, until golden brown. Remove with a slotted spoon and keep warm.

4. Add the remaining oil to the pan. Add the onions and cook, stirring occasionally, for 8–10 minutes, until lightly browned. Add the tomatoes, reduce the heat and cook, stirring occasionally, for 10–15 minutes, until thickened. Return the aubergines to the pan with the cheese and herbs. Stir well and remove the pan from the heat.

5. Preheat the grill and grease 2 gratin dishes with butter. Divide the aubergine mixture among the crêpes and roll up. Divide them between the dishes in a single layer, seam side down. Stir the mustard into the white sauce and pour it over the crêpes to cover.

6. Leave 1 dish to cool before freezing. Sprinkle the other with the Parmesan and cook under the preheated grill for about 5 minutes, until hot and the sauce is bubbling. Serve immediately with salad leaves.

Variation

* For ham and mushrooms crêpes, omit the aubergines and oil. Melt 55 g/2 oz butter in a frying pan and soften the onions for 5 minutes. Add 450 g/1 lb chopped mushrooms and cook for 5 minutes. Add 8 peeled and diced tomatoes, 225 g/8 oz diced ham and the herbs and cook for 5 minutes, then remove from the heat. (Do not add any cheese.) Fill the crêpes and stir the mustard and 280 g/ 10 oz grated cheese into the sauce.

To freeze/reheat

When cold, cover the reserved dish with clingfilm and foil or put into a freezer bag and freeze for up to 3 months. Thaw thoroughly, then sprinkle with 25 g/1 oz grated Parmesan cheese and bake in a preheated oven, 200°C/400°F/Gas Mark 6, for 30 minutes, until piping hot.

Classic Pizza

Also known as Margherita, this simple pizza is delicious as it is or as a basis for many other toppings. You can use ready-made pizza bases or make them using a packet mix.

· ·

2 x 30-cm/12-inch pizza bases

olive oil, for brushing and drizzling

700 ml/1¼ pints Tomato Sauce (see page 67)

280 g/10 oz mozzarella cheese, thinly sliced

4 tomatoes, thinly sliced

8 fresh basil leaves, torn

25 g/1 oz Parmesan cheese, grated

pepper

1. Preheat the oven to 220°C/425°F/Gas Mark 7. Put the pizza bases on baking sheets and brush with oil.

2. Divide the tomato sauce between the pizza bases, spreading it evenly over the surfaces and leaving a 1-cm/½-inch margin all around. Put overlapping slices of mozzarella and tomato over the top of each pizza, then sprinkle with the basil, Parmesan and pepper to taste.

3. Put 1 pizza in the refrigerator until ready to freeze. Drizzle the other with olive oil and bake in the preheated oven for 20 minutes, until crisp and golden brown. Serve immediately.

Variations

- For a mushroom topping, cook 1 finely chopped onion, 2 finely chopped garlic cloves and 450 g/1 lb sliced mushrooms in 3 tbsp olive oil over a low heat, stirring occasionally, for 8 minutes. Leave to cool before adding to the basic pizza.
- Add any of the following toppings: olives, capers, chargrilled peppers, anchovies, cooked peeled prawns and/ or sliced pepperoni.

To freeze/reheat

Open freeze the reserved uncooked pizza, then wrap in clingfilm and foil or put it into a freezer bag and store for up to 1 month. Thaw thoroughly, then transfer to a baking sheet, drizzle with oil and bake in a preheated oven, 220°C/425°F/ Gas Mark 7, for 20 minutes, until piping hot. You can bake the pizza from frozen for about 40 minutes.

Serves 4 + 4

1.25 kg/2 lb 12 oz canned chickpeas, drained and rinsed

3 garlic cloves, chopped

3 spring onions, chopped

2 fresh red chillies, deseeded and sliced

1½ tsp ground cumin

1½ tsp ground coriander

2 tbsp chopped fresh parsley

2 tbsp chopped fresh mint

2 eggs, lightly beaten

115–140 g/4–5 oz sesame seeds

vegetable oil, for shallow-frying

salt and pepper

To Serve

warmed pitta breads

salad

natural yogurt mixed with ground cumin and chopped fresh mint

Falafel

These spicy chickpea patties are incredibly tasty and are sure to become a family favourite. You could soak dried chickpeas and simmer them for 2 hours, but canned chickpeas are quicker.

1. Put the chickpeas, garlic, spring onions, chillies, cumin, coriander, parsley, mint and eggs into a food processor. Season to taste with salt and pepper, then pulse until the mixture forms a coarse paste.

2. Scrape the paste into a bowl and, if there is time, cover and chill in the refrigerator for 30 minutes.

3. Shape the mixture into 16 patties with your hands. Spread out the sesame seeds in a shallow dish and roll the falafel in them to coat. Put half the patties in the refrigerator until ready to freeze.

4. Pour just enough oil to cover the base into a large frying pan and heat. Add the falafel, in batches if necessary, and fry for 3–4 minutes on each side, until golden brown. Remove with a fish slice and drain on kitchen paper. Serve immediately in warmed pitta breads with salad and natural yogurt mixed with ground cumin and chopped fresh mint.

Variations

- Add 400 g/14 oz cooked chopped carrots to the mixture and substitute fresh coriander for the mint.
- Add 400 g/14 oz fresh (not frozen) broad beans to the mixture.
- Substitute canned haricot or cooked dried broad beans for the chickpeas.

To freeze/reheat

Pack the reserved uncooked falafel, interleaved with greaseproof paper, into a freezer bag and freeze for up to 3 months. Thaw thoroughly, then cook as described in step 4.

Mixed Bean Gratin

Filling, nourishing, colourful, tasty, quick and economical – what could be better? You can use any combination of canned beans you like or make the gratin with just one favourite type.

2 tbsp olive oil

2 onions, chopped

4 garlic cloves, finely chopped

800 g/1 lb 12 oz canned kidney beans, drained and rinsed

800 g/1 lb 12 oz canned cannellini beans, drained and rinsed

800 g/1 lb 12 oz canned flageolets beans, drained and rinsed

2 tbsp chopped fresh savory or 3 tbsp chopped fresh parsley

150 ml/5 fl oz crème fraîche

225 g/8 oz fresh breadcrumbs

115 g/4 oz Cheddar cheese, grated

25 g/1 oz butter or margarine, diced

salt and pepper

1. Preheat the oven to 180°C/350°F/Gas Mark 4. Heat the oil in a saucepan. Add the onions and garlic and cook over a low heat, stirring occasionally, for 5 minutes, until softened.

2. Add the beans, savory and crème fraîche. Season to taste with salt and pepper and cook, stirring occasionally, for 10 minutes.

3. Transfer the bean mixture to 2 gratin dishes, dividing it equally between them. Mix together the breadcrumbs and cheese in a bowl and sprinkle evenly over the bean mixture. Leave 1 dish to cool, then chill in the refrigerator until ready to freeze. Dot the butter over the surface of the other dish and bake in the preheated oven for about 20 minutes, until the topping is golden brown and crisp. Serve immediately.

Variations

- For bean and mushroom gratin, substitute 450 g/1 lb chopped mushrooms for the kidney beans.
- For spicy bean gratin, add 2 deseeded and chopped fresh red chillies and 1½ tbsp finely chopped fresh ginger to the pan in step 1. Substitute black-eyed beans for the kidney beans and aduki beans for the flageolets and stir 1½ tsp each ground cumin and coriander into the crème fraîche.

To freeze/reheat

Wrap the reserved dish in clingfilm and foil or put into a freezer bag and freeze for up to 3 months. Thaw thoroughly, then dot with 25 g/1 oz butter and bake in a preheated oven, 200°C/400°F/ Gas Mark 6, for 20–30 minutes, until piping hot and the topping is golden brown.

Spinach & Feta Pastries

Crisp filo encloses a melt-in-the-mouth filling flavoured with warm spices. Served with a Greek salad, these tasty parcels make a fabulous summery main course. Make sure you use filo dough from the chiller cabinet, not the freezer.

1.3 kg/3 lb spinach, coarse stalks removed

3 tbsp olive oil, plus extra for brushing

650 g/1 lb 7 oz white onions, chopped

4 garlic cloves, finely chopped

1 tsp ground cinnamon

1 tsp ground cumin

1 bunch of fresh parsley, finely chopped

100 g/3½ oz pine kernels, toasted

650 g/1 lb 7 oz feta cheese, crumbled

2 large eggs, lightly beaten

16 sheets filo pastry

salt and pepper

1. Put the spinach into a large saucepan with just the water clinging to its leaves after washing and cook, stirring occasionally, for 5–10 minutes, until wilted. Drain and squeeze out as much liquid as possible, then chop.

2. Heat the oil in a frying pan. Add the onions, garlic, cinnamon and cumin and cook over a low heat, stirring occasionally, for 5 minutes, until softened. Remove from the heat and transfer the mixture to a bowl. Stir in the parsley, pine kernels, cheese and eggs and mix until thoroughly combined.

3. Preheat the oven to 200°C/400°F/Gas Mark 6. Brush 2 baking sheets with oil. Cover the sheets of filo with a damp tea towel and take them out 2 at a time to prevent them from drying out. Brush 2 sheets with oil, put 1 on top of the other and halve lengthways.

4. Put about 4 tablespoons of the spinach and cheese mixture onto the end of each strip. Fold the corner point of the filo up and over the filling towards the left edge to make a triangular shape. Fold the bottom left-hand corner up to give a straight edge, then continue to roll up into a triangle. Brush with oil and put onto a prepared baking sheet. Continue making triangles in this way until all the ingredients have been used and you have 16 triangles (8 on each baking sheet).

5. Cover 1 baking sheet and put it into the refrigerator until ready to freeze. Put the other baking sheet into the preheated oven and bake for 15 minutes, until the pastries are golden brown. Serve immediately.

Variations

- Substitute chopped leeks for the onions and Stilton or another blue cheese for the feta.
- Drain and flake 800 g/1 lb 12 oz canned salmon, removing the skin and any bones. Pour 850 ml/1½ pints White Sauce (see page 6) into a bowl and stir in the salmon, 650 g/ 1 lb 7 oz drained canned asparagus tips and 2 tbsp chopped fresh dill. Make triangles with the salmon filling and filo and bake as described in step 5.

To freeze/reheat

Stack the reserved uncooked pastries, interleaved with greaseproof paper, and put into a freezer bag or wrap in clingfilm, then freeze for up to 3 months. Thaw thoroughly, then brush with oil. Place on an oiled baking sheet and bake in a preheated oven, 200°C/400°F/Gas Mark 6, for 20 minutes, until piping hot.

Vegetable Cassoulet

Haricot beans are the key ingredient of this French dish, although traditional versions also include some meat and/or sausages for extra flavour. In this version, fresh vegetables, tomatoes and mushrooms make this a tasty treat.

650 g/1 lb 7 oz dried haricot beans, soaked overnight in water to cover and drained

2 bay leaves

3 onions

4 cloves

1 tbsp olive oil

4 garlic cloves, finely chopped

4 leeks, sliced

800 g/1 lb 12 oz baby carrots

225 g/8 oz button mushrooms

800 g/1 lb 12 oz canned chopped tomatoes

4 tbsp chopped fresh parsley

1 tbsp chopped fresh savory

115 g/4 oz fresh breadcrumbs

salt and pepper

1. Put the beans and bay leaves into a saucepan. Stud 1 onion with the cloves and add to the pan. Pour in enough water to cover and bring to the boil. Reduce the heat, cover and simmer for 1 hour, then drain, reserving the cooking liquid. Remove and discard the bay leaves and onion.

2. Preheat the oven to 180°C/350°F/Gas Mark 4. Chop the remaining onions. Heat the oil in a flameproof casserole, then add the onions, garlic and leeks and cook over a low heat, stirring occasionally, for 5 minutes, until softened.

3. Add the carrots, mushrooms and tomatoes, pour in 850 ml/1½ pints of the reserved cooking liquid and season to taste with salt and pepper. Bring to the boil, then reduce the heat, cover and simmer for 15 minutes.

4. Stir in the beans, parsley and savory and taste and adjust the seasoning, adding salt and pepper if needed. Transfer half the cassoulet to a bowl and leave to cool before freezing. Sprinkle the surface of the remaining cassoulet with the breadcrumbs and transfer the casserole to the preheated oven. Bake, uncovered, for 40–45 minutes, until the topping is golden brown. Serve immediately.

Variations

- Omit the breadcrumbs and top the cassoulet with 8 slices of French bread each sprinkled with 1 tbsp grated cheese.
- For a more colourful mixture, substitute soaked kidney beans for half the haricot beans. Put them into a separate saucepan and bring to the boil, then boil vigorously for 15 minutes. Remove from the heat and drain, then return to the pan, pour in fresh water to cover and bring to the boil again. Reduce the heat, cover and simmer for 1½ hours.

To freeze/reheat

When cold, transfer the reserved cassoulet to a freezerproof container and freeze for up to 3 months. Thaw thoroughly, then transfer to a casserole and sprinkle with 115 g/4 oz fresh breadcrumbs. Bake, uncovered, in a preheated oven, 180°C/350°F/Gas Mark 4, for 40–45 minutes, until piping hot.

Serves 4 + 4

Ratatouille

This colourful dish from southern France is wonderfully adaptable and you can use a wide variety of seasonal vegetables to make the most of low prices. It is equally good served hot or at room temperature, perhaps with some crusty bread.

1 red pepper, quartered

1 orange pepper, quartered

1 green pepper, quartered

550 g/1 lb 4 oz aubergines, thickly sliced

2 tbsp olive oil, plus extra for brushing

2 large onions, sliced

3 garlic cloves, finely chopped

450 g/1 lb courgettes, thickly sliced

850 g/1 lb 14 oz tomatoes, peeled, deseeded and chopped

1½ tsp herbes de Provence

2 bay leaves

salt and pepper

1. Preheat the grill. Put the pepper quarters, skin side up, on a baking sheet and grill until charred and blistered. Remove with tongs, put them into a plastic bag, tie the top and leave to cool. Meanwhile, spread out the aubergine slices on the baking sheet, brush with oil and grill for 5 minutes, until lightly browned. Turn, brush with oil and grill for a further 5 minutes, until lightly browned. Remove with tongs.

2. Remove the peppers from the bag and peel off the skins. Remove and discard the seeds and membranes and cut the flesh into strips. Dice the aubergine slices.

3. Heat the oil in a large saucepan or flameproof casserole. Add the onions and cook over a low heat, stirring occasionally, for 8–10 minutes, until lightly browned. Add the garlic and courgettes and cook, stirring occasionally, for a further 10 minutes.

4. Stir in the peppers, aubergines, tomatoes, herbes de Provence and bay leaves. Season to taste with salt and pepper, then cover and simmer over a very low heat, stirring occasionally, for 25 minutes. Remove the lid and simmer, stirring occasionally, for a further 25–35 minutes, until the vegetables are tender.

5. Remove and discard the bay leaves. Transfer half the ratatouille to a bowl and leave to cool completely, then transfer to the refrigerator until ready to freeze. Serve the remaining ratatouille immediately, if serving hot, or leave to cool, if serving at room temperature.

Variations

- If the tomatoes are not very ripe or flavourful, stir in 2 tbsp sun-dried tomato paste mixed with 4 tbsp water with them. Alternatively, substitute 550 g/1 lb 4 oz canned chopped tomatoes.
- You can also use hot ratatouille to fill crêpes (see page 7) or top baked potatoes, and cooled ratatouille to fill warm tortilla wraps.

To freeze/reheat

Transfer the reserved ratatouille to a freezerproof container and freeze for up to 3 months. Thaw thoroughly, then leave to stand at room temperature for at least 30 minutes before serving cold or transfer to a saucepan and reheat gently for 15 minutes, until piping hot.

Chapter 4
Twice as Nice

71

75

77

Meatballs

A perennial family favourite, meatballs are easy to make and can be used in a number of ways. Here, they are served on a bed of pasta with a rich tomato sauce – which is also very versatile – and in a hearty casserole packed with vegetables.

Basic Recipe Serves 4 + 4

2 slices of bread, crusts removed

3 tbsp milk

600 g/1 lb 5 oz fresh steak mince

4 tbsp chopped fresh parsley

1 large egg

salt and pepper

1. Tear the bread into pieces and put it into a bowl. Pour in the milk and leave to soak for 5 minutes.
2. Put the steak, parsley and egg into a bowl. Squeeze out the bread and add it to the bowl, then season to taste with salt and pepper and mix well until thoroughly combined.
3. Dampen your hands and shape the mixture into 32 small balls. Put them onto a plate, cover and chill in the refrigerator for 30 minutes to firm up.
4. Use half the meatballs immediately and chill the remainder until ready to freeze.

Further variations

- Substitute chicken or turkey mince for the steak mince.
- Do not fry the meatballs but make the tomato sauce (see below) in a flameproof casserole and simmer for 20 minutes. Wrap each meatball in a slice of prosciutto, add to the casserole, cover and bake in a preheated oven, 180°C/350°F/Gas Mark 4, for 30 minutes. Serve with boiled rice.

To freeze/reheat

Transfer the reserved meatballs to a freezerproof container, interleaving the layers with greaseproof paper, and freeze for up to 3 months. Thaw thoroughly, then use as described below.

1 Meatballs in Tomato Sauce Serves 4

2 tbsp olive oil

½ quantity Meatballs

freshly cooked spaghetti and Parmesan cheese shavings, to serve

Tomato Sauce

2 tbsp olive oil

1 onion, chopped

2 garlic cloves, finely chopped

800 g/1 lb 12 oz canned chopped tomatoes

3 tbsp tomato purée

1 tsp sugar

1 tbsp chopped mixed fresh herbs

salt and pepper

1. Heat the oil in a frying pan. Add the meatballs, in batches if necessary, and cook over a medium heat, stirring and turning frequently, until browned all over. Remove from the pan and set aside.

2. For the tomato sauce, heat the oil in a saucepan. Add the onion and garlic and cook over a low heat, stirring occasionally, for 5 minutes. Add the tomatoes, tomato purée, sugar and herbs. Season to taste with salt and pepper and bring to the boil, stirring constantly.

3. Reduce the heat and gently stir in the meatballs. Partially cover the pan and simmer for 30–40 minutes, until the sauce has thickened and the meatballs are cooked through. Serve immediately with spaghetti and Parmesan cheese shavings.

2 Meatball Casserole Serves 4

2 tbsp olive oil

½ quantity Meatballs

2 Spanish onions, chopped

2 garlic cloves, finely chopped

500 g/1 lb 2 oz carrots, cut into pieces

500 g/1 lb 2 oz potatoes, cut into pieces

300 ml/10 fl oz beef stock or water

1 tbsp sweet paprika

500 ml/18 fl oz passata

salt and pepper

chopped fresh parsley, to garnish

1. Heat the oil in a large saucepan. Add the meatballs, in batches if necessary, and cook over a medium heat, stirring and turning frequently, until browned all over. Remove from the pan and set aside.

2. Add the onions and garlic to the pan and cook over a low heat, stirring occasionally, for 5 minutes. Add the carrots and potatoes, then pour in the stock and bring to the boil. Reduce the heat, cover and simmer for 15 minutes.

3. Sprinkle in the paprika, stir in the passata and return the meatballs to the pan. Re-cover the pan and simmer for a further 15–20 minutes. Season to taste with salt and pepper, garnish with parsley and serve immediately.

Bolognese Sauce

Known in Italy as ragù and traditionally served with tagliatelle, this meat sauce also features in lasagne al forno and may be served in a wide variety of ways, including as a stuffing for baked peppers.

Basic Recipe Serves 4 + 4

4 tbsp olive oil

175 g/6 oz bacon, diced

2 onions, finely chopped

4 garlic cloves, finely chopped

2 celery sticks, finely chopped

2 carrots, finely chopped

1 kg/2 lb 4 oz fresh steak mince

175 ml/6 fl oz red wine or beef stock

600 g/1 lb 5 oz canned chopped tomatoes

2 bay leaves

pinch of dried oregano

salt and pepper

1. Heat the oil in a large saucepan. Add the bacon and cook over a low heat, stirring frequently, for 5 minutes. Add the onions, garlic, celery and carrots and cook, stirring occasionally, for 5 minutes.

2. Add the steak, increase the heat to medium and cook, breaking up the meat with a wooden spoon, for 10 minutes, until lightly browned. Pour in the wine and cook for a few minutes, until the alcohol has evaporated. Stir in the tomatoes, add the bay leaves and oregano and season to taste with salt and pepper.

3. Bring to the boil, then reduce the heat, cover and simmer for 45 minutes. Remove the pan from the heat and leave to cool. Remove and discard the bay leaves. Use half the sauce immediately and chill the remainder until ready to freeze.

Further variations

- Reheat the sauce and serve tossed with freshly cooked pasta and sprinkled with grated Parmesan cheese.
- For stuffed tomatoes, substitute 8 large tomatoes for the peppers. Cut off the tops and carefully scoop out the seeds. Sprinkle the insides with salt and leave to drain, upside down, on kitchen paper, for 30 minutes. Pat dry, then fill and cook for 20 minutes as described below.

To freeze/reheat

When cold, transfer the reserved sauce to a freezerproof container and freeze for up to 3 months. Thaw thoroughly, then use as described below.

1 Lasagne al Forno Serves 4

225 g/8 oz lasagne sheets

pinch of grated nutmeg

2 tsp Dijon mustard

140 g/5 oz Cheddar or Gruyère cheese, grated

300 ml/10 fl oz hot White Sauce (see page 6)

½ quantity Bolognese Sauce

115 g/4 oz Parmesan cheese, grated, plus extra for sprinkling

fresh basil sprig, to garnish

1. Preheat the oven to 190°C/375°F/Gas Mark 5. If necessary, pre-cook the lasagne in boiling water according to the packet instructions, then drain.

2. Stir the nutmeg, mustard and Cheddar into the hot white sauce.

3. Make alternating layers of Bolognese sauce, lasagne, white sauce and Parmesan cheese in an ovenproof dish, finishing with a layer of white sauce and a sprinkling of Parmesan. Bake in the preheated oven for 30 minutes, until golden brown and bubbling. Leave to stand for 10 minutes, then garnish with a basil sprig and serve.

2 Stuffed Peppers Serves 4

4 large red, yellow or green peppers

25 g/1 oz butter

500 g/1 lb 2 oz tomatoes, peeled, deseeded and chopped

1 tbsp tomato purée

200 ml/7 fl oz beef stock

pinch of sugar

½ quantity Bolognese Sauce

salt and pepper

1. Cut the tops off the peppers and carefully scoop out the seeds and membranes without piercing the 'shells'. Blanch the shells and tops in a pan of boiling water for 2 minutes, then remove, drain upside down on kitchen paper and leave to cool.

2. Meanwhile, preheat the oven to 190°C/375°F/Gas Mark 5. Melt the butter in a saucepan. Add the tomatoes and cook over a low–medium heat, stirring frequently, for 10–15 minutes, until pulpy. Stir in the tomato purée and stock and bring to the boil, stirring constantly. Simmer, stirring frequently, for 5 minutes, until thickened. Stir in the sugar, season to taste with salt and pepper and remove from the heat.

3. Divide the Bolognese sauce among the pepper shells and top with the 'lids'. Put the peppers into an ovenproof dish and pour around the tomato mixture. Cover with foil and bake in the preheated oven for 30 minutes. Serve immediately.

Beef Chilli

A real feast for those who love hot and spicy food, this beef chilli can be served with kidney beans and rice as the ever-popular Tex-Mex chilli con carne or wrapped in tortillas and baked with a spicy sauce for Mexican enchiladas.

Basic Recipe Serves 4 + 4

2 tbsp corn oil

2 onions, chopped

3 garlic cloves, chopped

1 kg/2 lb 4 oz fresh steak mince

4–6 fresh chillies, deseeded and chopped

1 tsp chilli powder, or to taste

pinch of sugar

800 g/1 lb 12 oz canned chopped tomatoes

1 tbsp tomato purée

salt and pepper

1. Heat the oil in a saucepan. Add the onions and garlic and cook over a low heat, stirring occasionally, for 5 minutes, until softened. Add the steak, increase the heat to medium and cook, breaking up the meat with a wooden spoon, for 8–10 minutes, until lightly browned.

2. Stir in the chillies, half the chilli powder and the sugar and cook for 2 minutes, then add the tomatoes and tomato purée. Season to taste with salt and pepper. Reduce the heat, cover and simmer for 30 minutes.

3. Taste and adjust the seasoning, adding more chilli powder if necessary. Use half the chilli immediately and leave the remainder to cool.

Further variation

- For a basic vegetarian chilli, omit the steak mince from the basic recipe. Cook the tomato mixture for 10 minutes in step 2, then pour in 300 ml/10 fl oz red wine and 850 ml/ 1½ pints vegetable stock. Bring to the boil, then add 225 g/8 oz red lentils, reduce the heat, cover and simmer, stirring occasionally, for 35 minutes, adding more liquid if necessary.

To freeze/reheat

When cold, transfer the reserved chilli to a freezerproof container and freeze for up to 3 months. Thaw thoroughly, then use as described below.

① Chilli con Carne Serves 4

½ quantity Beef Chilli

1 tsp ground cumin

400 g/14 oz canned red kidney beans, drained and rinsed

freshly cooked rice, to serve

chopped fresh coriander, to garnish

1. If necessary, reheat the beef chilli in a saucepan over a low heat, stirring occasionally. Stir in the cumin and kidney beans and simmer for 5–8 minutes, until heated through.
2. Serve immediately on a bed of rice, garnished with coriander.

② Baked Enchiladas Serves 4

2 dried chillies, such as ancho

1 tbsp chopped fresh coriander

1 small onion, chopped

1 garlic clove, chopped

280 g/10 oz tomatoes, peeled, deseeded and coarsely chopped

1 tbsp corn oil

150 ml/5 fl oz soured cream

½ quantity Beef Chilli

8 flour tortillas, warmed

40 g/1½ oz Parmesan cheese, grated

salt and pepper

herb salad, to serve

1. Dry-fry the chillies in a heavy-based frying pan over a medium heat, stirring frequently, for 1 minute. Remove from the heat and leave to cool, then halve and deseed. Tear up the chillies and put them into a bowl. Pour in enough warm water to cover and leave to soak for 15 minutes. Drain, reserving the soaking water.
2. Put the chillies, 1 tablespoon of the soaking water, the coriander, onion, garlic and tomatoes into a food processor and process until smooth.
3. Heat the oil in a frying pan. Add the chilli and tomato mixture and cook over a low heat, stirring constantly, for 4–5 minutes. Stir in the soured cream and season to taste with salt and pepper. Remove the pan from the heat.
4. Preheat the oven to 180°C/350°F/Gas Mark 4. Put the beef chilli into a saucepan and reheat gently, if necessary, stirring occasionally.
5. Spoon some of the beef chilli in a line along the centre of a tortilla and roll up. Put the rolled tortilla, seam side down, into an ovenproof dish. Repeat with the remaining tortillas and beef chilli. Pour the sauce over them, sprinkle with the cheese and bake in the preheated oven for 20 minutes. Serve immediately with herb salad.

Shallot & Pine Kernel Stuffing

Keep a supply of this simple stuffing in the freezer for an easy way to turn boring chicken breasts into crisp filled pockets or make the meat go further when the household budget is running low with tasty beef olives.

Basic Recipe Serves 4 + 4

25 g/1 oz butter

4 shallots, chopped

55 g/2 oz pine kernels

25 g/1 oz fresh breadcrumbs

2 tbsp chopped fresh parsley

55 g/2 oz Gruyère cheese, grated

2 egg yolks

salt and pepper

1. Melt the butter in a frying pan. Add the shallots and cook over a low heat, stirring occasionally, for 5 minutes, until softened.

2. Remove the pan from the heat and leave to cool. Mix together the shallots, pine kernels, breadcrumbs, parsley, cheese and egg yolks in a bowl and season to taste with salt and pepper.

3. Use half the stuffing immediately and chill the remainder until ready to freeze.

Further variation

- For a simpler chicken dish, make 3 diagonal slashes on each chicken breast and fill with the stuffing. Wrap each chicken breast in 1–2 slices prosciutto and cook in an oiled griddle pan, turning once or twice, for 20–25 minutes, until cooked through and tender.

To freeze/reheat

Transfer the reserved stuffing to a freezerproof container and freeze for up to 1 month. Thaw thoroughly, then use as described below.

❶ Crisp Chicken Pockets Serves 4

55 g/2 oz bacon, diced

55 g/2 oz fresh breadcrumbs

1 tbsp chopped fresh parsley

1½ tbsp grated Parmesan cheese

4 skinless, boneless chicken breasts

½ quantity Shallot & Pine Kernel Stuffing

25 g/1 oz butter, plus extra for greasing

1 tbsp wholegrain mustard

1 tbsp clear honey

olive oil, for drizzling

salad leaves, to serve

1. Preheat the oven to 200°C/400°F/Gas Mark 6. Grease an ovenproof dish. Dry-fry the bacon in a heavy-based frying pan over a medium heat, stirring frequently, for a few minutes, until crisp. Remove with a slotted spoon and mix with the breadcrumbs, parsley and Parmesan in a bowl.

2. Using a sharp knife, cut a pocket in each of the chicken breasts, then divide the stuffing among them, packing it well down. Put the chicken breasts into the prepared dish.

3. Melt the butter, then stir in the mustard and honey. Brush over the chicken, then press on the bacon mixture. Drizzle over a little oil.

4. Bake in the preheated oven for 35–40 minutes, until the chicken is cooked through and the topping is crisp. Serve immediately with salad leaves.

❷ Beef Olives Serves 4

8 slices of top rump frying steak

½ quantity Shallot & Pine Kernel Stuffing

4 tbsp olive oil

1 onion, sliced

1 carrot, sliced

150 ml/5 fl oz red wine (or use extra beef stock)

1 tsp cornflour

300 ml/10 fl oz beef stock

1 bay leaf

salt and pepper

freshly cooked asparagus, to serve

1. Put each slice of steak between 2 sheets of clingfilm and beat with the flat side of a meat hammer until flattened and even. Divide the stuffing among the pieces of meat, spreading it evenly. Roll up and secure with string.

2. Preheat the oven to 160°C/325°F/Gas Mark 3. Heat the oil in a flameproof casserole. Add the onion and beef olives and cook over a low–medium heat, stirring and turning occasionally, for 5–8 minutes, until the meat is lightly browned and the onion is softened.

3. Add the carrot and cook for 3–4 minutes, then pour in the wine and cook until the alcohol has evaporated. Mix the cornflour to a paste with a little of the stock and set aside. Pour the remaining stock into the casserole, add the bay leaf, season well with salt and pepper and cook for a few minutes.

4. Cover the casserole, transfer to the preheated oven and cook for 1½–2 hours, until the meat is tender. Remove and discard the string and transfer the beef olives to a serving dish. Stir the reserved cornflour paste into the cooking liquid and simmer, stirring constantly, for 5–10 minutes, until thickened. Pour the sauce over the beef olives and serve immediately with asparagus.

Roasted Vegetables

Roasting vegetables gives them a delicious sweetness and all the delicious flavours meld together. As well as serving them as a straightforward accompaniment, you can use them to make a fabulous strudel or a tasty base for baked eggs.

Basic Recipe Serves 4 + 4

2 red onions, sliced

1 large aubergine, diced

4 red peppers, deseeded and sliced

4 courgettes, diced

4 tomatoes, peeled and coarsely chopped

3 garlic cloves, chopped

2 fresh parsley sprigs

2 fresh rosemary sprigs

3 tbsp olive oil

4 tbsp sultanas

4 tbsp pine kernels

salt and pepper

1. Preheat the oven to 180°C/350°F/Gas Mark 4.

2. Put the onions, aubergine, red peppers, courgettes, tomatoes, garlic, parsley and rosemary into 2 roasting tins. Pour over the oil and toss well. Roast in the preheated oven, stirring occasionally, for 40–45 minutes, covering with foil if beginning to burn.

3. Remove the tins from the oven and leave to cool. Remove and discard the herbs. Stir in the sultanas and pine kernels and season lightly with salt and pepper.

4. Use half the roasted vegetables immediately and chill the remainder until ready to freeze.

Further variations

- Use the roasted vegetables as a filling for omelettes or a topping for pasta.
- For a vegetable lasagne, substitute the roasted vegetables for the Bolognese sauce in Lasagne al Forno (see page 69).

To freeze/reheat

When cold, transfer the reserved roasted vegetables to a freezerproof container and freeze for up to 2 months. Thaw thoroughly, then use as described below.

1 Roasted Vegetable Strudel Serves 4

8 sheets filo pastry, each measuring about 30 x 18 cm/12 x 7 inches

55 g/2 oz butter, melted, plus extra for greasing

½ quantity Roasted Vegetables

115 g/4 oz Taleggio or fontina cheese, diced

salad leaves, to serve

1. Preheat the oven to 190°C/375°F/Gas Mark 5. Grease a baking sheet with butter.

2. Put 2 sheets of filo pastry side by side, overlapping by 5 cm/2 inches, and brush with the melted butter. Cover with 2 more overlapping sheets and brush with melted butter, then repeat with 2 more layers of 2 sheets each, brushing with melted butter.

3. Spoon the roasted vegetables along one long side of the dough rectangle and sprinkle with the cheese. Roll up into a cylinder.

4. Transfer to the prepared baking sheet and brush with the remaining melted butter. Bake in the preheated oven for 30–35 minutes, until golden brown. Remove from the oven and leave to stand for 5 minutes, then cut into slices and serve with salad leaves.

2 Eggs in Nests Serves 4

butter, for greasing

½ quantity Roasted Vegetables

4 eggs

salt and white pepper

chopped fresh chervil, to garnish

1. Preheat the oven to 180°C/350°F/Gas Mark 4. Grease 4 individual baking dishes or a single large ovenproof dish with butter.

2. Divide the roasted vegetables evenly among the dishes, cover with foil and bake in the preheated oven for 10 minutes. Remove from the oven and uncover the dishes. Make a shallow hollow in the centre of each dish with the back of a spoon. Break an egg into each hollow and season to taste with salt and white pepper.

3. Re-cover the dishes with foil, return to the oven and bake for a further 15 minutes, until the eggs are just set.

4. Remove from the oven and discard the foil. Sprinkle with chervil and serve immediately.

Sticky Chilli Chicken

Marinated in Thai flavourings and then grilled, this piquant chicken is fabulous served hot with pad Thai noodles or cold with a crisp salad and an exotic dressing. It's just the thing when you don't want to spend much time in the kitchen.

Basic Recipe Serves 4 + 4

juice and grated rind of 2 limes
2 garlic cloves, finely chopped
6 tbsp sweet chilli sauce
8 chicken breast fillets or 16 chicken thigh fillets

1. Mix together the lime juice and rind, garlic and sweet chilli sauce in a dish. Add the chicken, turning to coat, and leave to marinate, turning occasionally, for at least 30 minutes.

2. Preheat the grill. Remove the chicken from the marinade and put it on a baking sheet, skin side down, and flatten gently with your hand. Grill for 4–5 minutes, then turn and grill for a further 4–5 minutes, until the skin is crisp.

3. Use half the chicken immediately, either hot or cold, and leave the remainder to cool.

Further variations

- Substitute a meaty fish steak or fillet, such as tuna, for the chicken and grill for 2–3 minutes on each side.
- For a simpler noodle accompaniment, cook the noodles according to the packet instructions, drain and toss with 2 tbsp lime juice and 2 tbsp chopped fresh coriander.

To freeze/reheat

When cold, transfer the reserved chicken to a freezerproof container and freeze for up to 3 months. Thaw thoroughly and bring to room temperature, then use as described below.

① Sticky Chicken with Pad Thai Noodles Serves 4

3 tbsp groundnut oil

3 garlic cloves, finely chopped

200 g/7 oz raw prawns, peeled and deveined

2 eggs, lightly beaten

300 g/10½ oz rice noodles, soaked in warm water for 20 minutes and drained

140 g/5 oz fresh beansprouts

3 tbsp Thai fish sauce

1 tbsp sugar

1 tbsp dark soy sauce

1 tbsp lime juice

pinch of dried chilli flakes

½ quantity hot Sticky Chilli Chicken

2 tbsp chopped fresh coriander

lime wedges, to garnish

1. Heat 1 tablespoon of the oil in a wok or large frying pan. Add the garlic and stir-fry over a high heat for 30 seconds. Add the prawns and stir-fry for 2 minutes, then remove from the pan.

2. Add 1 tablespoon of the remaining oil to the wok. Add the eggs and tilt the wok to cover the base. Cook, stirring to break into small pieces, until lightly set. Remove from the wok and set aside.

3. Add the remaining oil to the wok. Add the noodles and stir-fry for 2–3 minutes. Add the beansprouts, fish sauce, sugar, soy sauce, lime juice and chilli flakes and cook, stirring and tossing, for a further 3–4 minutes, until heated through.

4. Return the prawns and eggs to the wok and mix well. Divide the noodle mixture among plates and top with the chicken. Sprinkle with coriander and serve immediately with lime wedges.

② Thai Chicken Salad Serves 4

125 ml/4 fl oz coconut cream

2 tbsp light brown sugar

2 tbsp Thai fish sauce

2 tbsp lime juice

4 shallots, thinly sliced

1 tsp finely chopped fresh galangal or ginger

4 spring onions, shredded

1 fresh red chilli, deseeded and finely chopped

10 fresh mint leaves, torn

55 g/2 oz roasted cashew nuts

½ quantity cold Sticky Chilli Chicken, sliced

salad leaves, to serve

1. Pour the coconut cream into a saucepan and add the sugar, fish sauce and lime juice. Heat gently, stirring until the sugar has dissolved, then remove from the heat.

2. Mix together the shallots, galangal, spring onions, chilli, mint, cashew nuts and chicken in a bowl. Pour the coconut dressing over the mixture and toss gently. Serve immediately on a bed of salad leaves.

Foolproof Fish

Fish is an important part of a healthy diet but it is sometimes difficult to persuade the family to eat it and inexperienced cooks are often unsure quite what to do with it. Use this easy basic recipe to make two very different, equally impressive dishes.

Basic Recipe Serves 4 + 4

500 g/1 lb 2 oz potatoes, cut into chunks

650 g/1 lb 7 oz white fish fillets, skinned

300 ml/10 fl oz milk

4 egg yolks

2 garlic cloves, finely chopped

3 tbsp chopped fresh parsley

grated rind and juice of 1 lemon

salt and pepper

1. Put the potatoes into a large saucepan, pour in water to cover, add a pinch of salt and bring to the boil. Reduce the heat, cover and simmer for 20–25 minutes, until tender but not disintegrating.

2. Meanwhile, put the fish into a separate large saucepan, pour in the milk and season to taste with salt and pepper. Bring just to the boil, then reduce the heat and poach gently for 10–12 minutes, until the flesh flakes easily. Remove the pan from the heat, lift out the fish with a fish slice and reserve the cooking liquid.

3. Drain the potatoes and transfer to a bowl. Mash well, adding as much of the reserved cooking liquid as required for a creamy mixture. Beat in the egg yolks, garlic, parsley, lemon rind and lemon juice and season to taste with salt and pepper.

4. Flake the fish, removing any pin bones, and stir it into the potato mixture. Use half the fish mixture immediately and leave the remainder to cool.

❶ Fish Soufflé Serves 4

butter, for greasing

2 egg whites

½ quantity Foolproof Fish

140 g/5 oz cooked peeled prawns

55 g/2 oz Cheddar cheese, grated

1. Preheat the oven to 200°C/400°F/Gas Mark 6. Grease a gratin dish with butter.

2. Whisk the egg whites in a grease-free bowl until stiff. Gently mix together the fish mixture and prawns in a separate bowl, then fold in the egg whites. Spoon the mixture into the prepared dish.

3. Sprinkle with the cheese and bake in the preheated oven for 25 minutes, until golden brown and just set. Serve immediately.

❷ Crispy Fish Fritters Serves 4

85 g/3 oz self-raising flour, plus extra for dusting

pinch of salt

1 egg

2 tsp olive oil

150 ml/5 fl oz water

½ quantity Foolproof Fish

groundnut oil, for deep-frying

lemon wedges and parsley sprigs, to garnish

tartare sauce, to serve

1. Sift the flour and salt into a bowl and beat in the egg, olive oil and water to make a batter.

2. Dust your hands with flour, then scoop up small pieces of the fish mixture and shape into 24 balls.

3. Heat the groundnut oil in a deep-fat fryer to 180–190°C/350–375°F, or until a cube of bread browns in 30 seconds.

4. Dip the balls into the batter to coat, draining off any excess. Deep-fry the fritters, in batches if necessary, for 4–5 minutes, until golden brown. Remove with a slotted spoon and drain on kitchen paper.

5. Garnish with lemon wedges and parsley sprigs and serve with tartare sauce.

Chapter 5
Love your Leftovers

86

88

92

Serves 4

Italian Bread Soup

Italians are the world's greatest experts at making the most of all leftovers and have a number of imaginative ways of using up stale bread. Good-quality rustic bread should never be wasted, so make it into this spicy soup.

● ●

1.5 litres/2¾ pints chicken stock

5 tbsp olive oil

2 garlic cloves, finely chopped

1 tsp crushed dried chillies

3 tbsp chopped fresh flat-leaf parsley

175 g/6 oz stale bread, coarsely chopped

grated Parmesan cheese, to serve

1. Pour the stock into a saucepan and bring just to the boil.

2. Meanwhile, heat the oil in a separate large saucepan. Add the garlic, chillies and parsley and cook, stirring constantly, for 1 minute. Add the bread and cook, stirring frequently, for 4 minutes, until lightly browned.

3. Pour in the hot stock, cover and simmer for 30 minutes, then remove from the heat. Serve immediately, sprinkled with Parmesan cheese, or leave to cool before freezing.

Variation

- Heat the oil as in step 2 and cook 2 finely chopped onions and 2 finely chopped garlic cloves over a low heat, stirring occasionally, for 8 minutes, until light golden. Add the bread and cook, stirring frequently, for 4 minutes, then stir in 1 deseeded and diced red pepper, 4 finely chopped celery sticks and 700 g/1 lb 9 oz chopped peeled tomatoes. Simmer, stirring occasionally, for 20 minutes. Pour in the hot stock, cover and simmer for 30 minutes.

To freeze/reheat

When cold, transfer the soup to a freezerproof container and freeze for up to 3 months. Thaw thoroughly, then reheat gently, stirring frequently, until piping hot.

Meal-in-a-bowl Soup

Perfect stock is made from raw ingredients but you can make a very good one using a cooked poultry carcass. There will be enough to make a delicious and filling soup for four and some to freeze for another day.

● ●

1 cooked chicken or turkey carcass, including any leftover meat and skin

2 onions

1 leek, chopped

2 carrots, chopped

1 garlic clove

1 bouquet garni

6 black peppercorns

1 tbsp olive oil

1 red pepper, deseeded and sliced

1 tsp ground cumin

1 tsp ground coriander

4 tbsp long-grain rice

400 g/14 oz canned gunga peas, chickpeas or haricot beans, drained

salt

chopped fresh coriander and sliced fresh red chilli, to garnish

1. Cut off any remaining meat from the carcass and dice. Cover and set aside in the refrigerator. Put all the bones, skin, jelly, wingtips and meat scraps into a large saucepan. Chop 1 of the onions.

2. Add the chopped onion, leek, carrots, garlic, bouquet garni and peppercorns to the pan. Pour in enough water to cover and gradually bring to the boil, skimming off any foam that rises to the surface. Reduce the heat and simmer very gently for 2 hours.

3. Remove the pan from the heat and strain through a muslin-lined strainer into a bowl, then leave to cool. When cold, skim off the fat with folded kitchen paper. Alternatively, if there is time, chill in the refrigerator overnight and lift off the fat that has solidified on the surface the next day.

4. Pour 1.5 litres/2¾ pints of the stock into a saucepan and heat gently. Return the remainder to the refrigerator until ready to freeze. Slice the remaining onion.

5. Heat the oil in a separate large saucepan. Add the sliced onion and cook over a low heat, stirring occasionally, for 5 minutes, until softened. Add the red pepper, cumin, ground coriander and rice and cook, stirring constantly, for 1 minute.

6. Pour in the hot stock, season to taste with salt and pepper and stir in the gunga peas and the reserved meat. Bring to the boil, reduce the heat, cover and simmer for 10 minutes, until the rice is tender. Serve immediately, garnished with coriander and red chilli, or leave to cool before freezing.

Variations

- You can add leftover cooked vegetables to the stock. Potatoes will tend to make it cloudy and any members of the cabbage family should be used cautiously as they are strongly flavoured, but others, such as carrots, beans, courgettes and peas, will contribute to the flavour of this quite mild stock.
- For a hotter flavour, add a pinch of chilli flakes, ½ tsp ground ginger and ½ tsp ground turmeric to the pan with the other spices.

To freeze/reheat

When cold, transfer the soup to a freezerproof container and freeze for up to 3 months. Thaw thoroughly, then pour into a saucepan and reheat gently, until piping hot. Freeze the stock in ice cube trays, then transfer to a freezer bag. Use from frozen for stews, sauces and other dishes.

Serves 4

Cheat's Moussaka

This Greek dish is normally made with fresh lamb mince, but here the traditional recipe has been adapted to use up leftover cooked lamb. While not authentic, it's still very tasty and – an extra bonus – quicker to cook.

55 g/2 oz butter

2 tbsp olive oil

2 aubergines, thinly sliced

4 potatoes, thinly sliced

2 onions, thinly sliced

2 garlic cloves, finely chopped

4 tomatoes, peeled and thinly sliced

500 g/1 lb 2 oz leftover cooked lamb, diced

pinch of grated nutmeg

1 quantity warm White Sauce (see page 6)

115 g/4 oz Cheddar cheese, grated

1 egg

55 g/2 oz Parmesan cheese, grated

salt and pepper

1. Melt half the butter with half the oil in a frying pan. Add the aubergine and potato slices and cook over a low–medium heat, stirring and turning frequently, for 8–10 minutes, until lightly browned. Remove with a fish slice.

2. Add the remaining butter and oil to the pan. Add the onions and garlic and cook over a low heat, stirring occasionally, for 5 minutes, until softened. Add the tomatoes and cook for a further 2 minutes. Stir in the lamb and remove the pan from the heat.

3. Stir the nutmeg into the white sauce, season to taste with salt and pepper and add the cheese, stirring until melted. Beat in the egg.

4. Make alternating layers of the aubergine and potato slices, the meat mixture and the sauce in an ovenproof dish, ending with a layer of the sauce to cover completely.

5. If you wish to freeze the dish, set it aside to cool. Otherwise, sprinkle the Parmesan over the top and bake in a preheated oven, 160°C/325°F/Gas Mark 3, for 45–55 minutes, until the topping is golden brown and bubbling. Serve immediately.

Variations

- You can substitute other leftover cooked meat, such as beef, pork or chicken, for the lamb.
- For more flavour, add 1 deseeded and finely chopped fresh chilli to the pan with the onions and garlic and stir in 1 tbsp chopped fresh marjoram with the tomatoes.
- Substitute thinly sliced courgettes for the aubergines.
- Substitute crumbled feta cheese for half the Cheddar.

To freeze/reheat

When cold, cover the dish with clingfilm and foil and freeze for up to 3 months. Thaw thoroughly, then sprinkle with 55 g/2 oz grated Parmesan cheese and bake in a preheated oven, 160°C/325°F/Gas Mark 3, for 45–55 minutes, until piping hot.

Gammon & Apple Pie

Gammon is delicious when served hot and is an ideal choice for a family gathering, but too often it appears cold the next day with salad – something of a disappointment after its former glory. Give it a makeover in this traditional pie.

butter, for greasing

2 potatoes, chopped

1 large onion, chopped

300–350 g/10½–12 oz leftover cooked gammon, diced

2 tart apples, peeled, cored and chopped

150 ml/5 fl oz water

½ quantity Shortcrust Pastry (see page 7) or 375 g/13 oz shop-bought shortcrust pastry

plain flour, for dusting

milk, for brushing

salt and pepper

1. Preheat the oven to 200°C/400°F/Gas Mark 6. Grease a pie dish with butter.

2. Put the potatoes into the base of the prepared dish and cover with the onion, seasoning each layer with salt and pepper to taste. Mix together the gammon and apples, season to taste with salt and pepper and spoon the mixture on top of the onion. Pour in the water.

3. Roll out the pastry on a lightly floured surface to about 5 cm/2 inches bigger than the dish. Cut a strip from around the edge and place it on the rim of the dish. Brush with water and carefully lift the remaining pastry on top of the pie, pressing all around the rim with your finger. Knock up the edge. Cut 2 small slits in the top of the pie and decorate with any pastry trimmings.

4. Brush the top of the pie with milk, put it onto a baking sheet and bake in the preheated oven for 30 minutes, until the pastry is golden brown. If you wish to freeze the dish, remove the pie from the oven and leave to cool. Otherwise, reduce the oven temperature to 160°C/325°F/ Gas Mark 3, cover the pastry with foil to prevent it from burning and bake for a further 30–35 minutes. Serve immediately.

Variations

- You can substitute leftover boiled bacon or roast pork for the gammon.
- If you have leftover vegetables, such as carrots or peas, add them between the onion and gammon layers.
- For extra flavour, substitute chicken stock or cider for the water.

To freeze/reheat

When cold, wrap the pie in clingfilm and foil and freeze for up to 3 months. Thaw thoroughly and unwrap the pie. Cover the pastry with foil to prevent it from burning and bake in a preheated oven, 160°C/325°F/Gas Mark 3, for 45–50 minutes, until piping hot. Serve immediately.

Serves 4

Salmon Terrine

A whole poached salmon is a popular choice for a festive lunch or a party buffet, but it quickly loses its elegant appearance and becomes a rather sad mangled mess. Nevertheless, there will be lots left over and it's far too good to waste.

400–450 g/14–16 oz poached salmon, flaked

1 quantity White Sauce (see page 6)

pinch of grated nutmeg

4 tbsp water

4 tsp powdered gelatine

2 tbsp double cream

salt and pepper

cucumber ribbons and rocket leaves, to serve

1. Line a 900-g/2-lb loaf tin with clingfilm. Mix together the salmon, white sauce and nutmeg in a bowl, stirring and mashing with a wooden spoon until smooth. Alternatively, process to a purée in a food processor or blender. Season to taste with salt and pepper.

2. Pour the water into a small heatproof bowl, sprinkle the gelatine over the surface and leave to soak for 5 minutes, until spongy. Put the bowl into a small saucepan of barely simmering water and heat until the gelatine has dissolved and the liquid is clear.

3. Stir the gelatine and cream into the fish mixture, then transfer to the prepared tin. Chill in the refrigerator for 2–3 hours, until set. If you wish to freeze the terrine, do so at this stage. Otherwise, run a knife around the tin, then quickly dip the base into hot water. Invert a serving plate over the tin, then reverse the two and turn out. Garnish with cucumber ribbons and rocket leaves and serve immediately.

Variations

- You can also use poached white fish instead of the salmon or a mixture of fish and cooked peeled prawns.
- If using leaf gelatine, you will need 2–3 leaves – check the instructions on the packet. Put them into a small bowl of cold water and leave for 5 minutes to soften, then squeeze out the excess liquid. Put them into a small heatproof bowl and put it into a pan of barely simmering water. Heat until the gelatine has dissolved completely.

To freeze/reheat

Wrap the tin in clingfilm and foil and freeze for up to 1 month. Thaw in the refrigerator for 12 hours.

Veggie Cakes

It seems a shame to throw away leftover vegetables but simply warming them to serve again is not very appetizing and there are rarely enough of them to serve everyone. Use them to make these scrumptious veggie cakes for another day.

175 g/6 oz leftover cooked vegetables, such as cabbage, spinach, Brussels sprouts, peas and/or carrots

700 g/1 lb 9 oz leftover boiled or mashed potatoes

6 tbsp olive oil

1 large onion, chopped

salt and pepper

rocket leaves, to garnish

tomato ketchup, to serve

1. Coarsely chop the vegetables to about the same size. If necessary, mash the potatoes.

2. Heat 4 tablespoons of the oil in a frying pan. Add the onion and cook over a low heat, stirring occasionally, for 8–10 minutes, until light golden brown. Add the chopped vegetables and cook, stirring frequently, for a further 5 minutes.

3. Transfer the onion and vegetable mixture to a bowl, add the mashed potatoes and mix well until thoroughly combined. Season to taste with salt and pepper.

4. Shape the mixture into 8 cakes, either with your hands or by spooning it into a 9-cm/3½-inch plain biscuit cutter, patting it down firmly and then removing the cutter.

5. Put the veggie cakes onto a plate, cover and chill in the refrigerator for 30 minutes to firm up. If you wish to freeze the veggie cakes, do so at this stage. Otherwise, heat the remaining oil in a large frying pan. Add the veggie cakes, in batches if necessary, and cook for 2–3 minutes on each side, until golden brown. Remove with a fish slice and transfer to serving plates. Garnish with rocket leaves and serve immediately with tomato ketchup.

Variations

- Substitute other leftover mashed root vegetables, such as swede, celeriac or sweet potatoes, for the potatoes or use a mixture.
- Serve the veggie cakes topped with a poached egg or a generous spoonful of scrambled egg.
- For additional flavour, add a pinch of grated nutmeg or chilli powder or 1 tbsp chopped fresh herbs to the potato and vegetable mixture in step 3.

To freeze/reheat

Carefully wrap the cakes individually in clingfilm, put them into a freezer bag and freeze for up to 1 month. Thaw thoroughly, then cook as described in step 5.

Serves 4

Cheesy Vegetable Bake

You can use virtually any leftover cooked vegetables, no matter how small the individual quantities, the last sprigs of almost any fresh herbs and any end pieces of still-edible cheese left in the refrigerator.

500 g/1 lb 2 oz leftover cooked vegetables, such as beans, peas, carrots, cauliflower, broccoli, courgettes, parsnips, potatoes and/or sweet potatoes

25 g/1 oz butter, plus extra for greasing

6 slices of bacon, diced

2 tart apples, peeled, cored and diced

2 tbsp chopped fresh herbs (optional)

115 g/4 oz Cheddar or other cheese, grated

½ quantity hot White Sauce (see page 6)

salt and pepper

1. Chop any large vegetables and cut cauliflower and broccoli, if using, into florets. Grease an ovenproof dish with butter.

2. Melt the butter in a frying pan. Add the bacon and cook over a medium heat, stirring frequently, for 5–6 minutes, until lightly browned. Remove from the heat.

3. Place the vegetables, bacon and apples in the prepared dish, sprinkling with herbs, if using, and seasoning with salt and pepper to taste.

4. Add the cheese to the white sauce and stir well until melted. Pour the sauce over the vegetables to cover completely. If you wish to freeze the dish, set it aside to cool. Otherwise, transfer to a preheated oven, 190°C/375°F/Gas Mark 5, and bake for 25–30 minutes, until the topping is golden brown and bubbling. Serve immediately.

Variations

- You can also incorporate any small quantities of leftover canned vegetables or beans.
- Substitute diced ham, leftover cooked minced meat or Bolognese Sauce (see page 68), diced salami or sliced leftover cooked sausages for the bacon.
- If you have ½ red or green pepper, 1 tomato, 2 celery sticks or any similar vegetables left in the refrigerator, chop and add them to the pan with the bacon.

To freeze/reheat

When cold, cover the dish with clingfilm and foil and freeze for up to 1 month. Thaw thoroughly, then bake in a preheated oven, 190°C/375°F/ Gas Mark 5, for 25–30 minutes, until piping hot.

Recipe Index

34 50 82

* Check the labels on ingredients, such as cheese, to ensure that they are suitable for vegetarians.